'BLUES BOY'

'BLUES BOY'

The Life and Music
of B. B. King

Sebastian Danchin

University Press of Mississippi   Jackson

Credits, photographic section

Delta Haze Corporaton © 1990, 1993, 1994, 1995, 1997:

Photos by Hooks Bros., figures 1–4

Photos by Ernest C. Withers, figures 6–12, 14, 16

Photo by Jim Marshall, figure 30

Photos by William R. Ferris, William R. Ferris Collection, Archives and Special Collections,
John D. Williams Library, University of Mississippi, figures 18–23, 28–29

Courtesy of Blues Archive, John D. Williams Library, University of Mississippi, figures 15, 31,
33–34, 36, 40

Photos by Sebastian Danchin, figures 5, 13, 24–27, 35, 38

Photos by Dick Waterman, figures 17, 32, 43

Photos by Penny Flautt Mayfield, figures 39, 41–42

Photo by John Webb, figure 37

Photos © David Rae Morris/Impact Visuals, 1986

Library of Congress Cataloging-in-Publication Data

Danchin, Sebastian.
    Blues Boy : the life and music of B.B. King / Sebastian Danchin.
        p.   cm.—(American made music series)
    Includes bibliographical references (p.   ), discography (p.   )
and index.
    ISBN 1-57806-017-6 (cloth : alk. paper)
    1. King, B. B.   2. Blues musicians—United States—Biography.
I. Title.   II. Series.
ML420.K473D36   1998
781.643'092—dc21
    [B]   97-9716
                                                                                  CIP
                                                                                   MN

British Library Cataloging-in-Publication data available

CONTENTS

Acknowledgments vii

Introduction ix

1 Indianola, Mississippi, Seeds (1925–1946) 1

2 Radio Days (1947–1951) 15

3 The Chitlin Circuit (1952–1960) 32

4 The Years of Uncertainty (1961–1966) 55

5 B. B. at the Fillmore (1966–1975) 72

6 The Plan Fulfilled (1975–1997) 89

7 Lucille 102

Epilogue 116

Notes 120

Selected Discography 127

Index 149

ACKNOWLEDGMENTS

The seed for this book was planted in 1976, on the occasion of my first prolonged stay in the United States. My good friend Eddie Boyd, who had made Europe his home a little over ten years before, had provided me with a list of names and telephone numbers which opened many doors for me. At the time, I conducted a large number of interviews for a book I was writing on the life of the late Earl Hooker; Earl was an astounding guitar player himself, and quite naturally the name of B. B. King would often crop up in the conversations I had with Chicago musicians.

My first encounter with B. B. should have happened the following year, but fate prevented it. I had booked various acts for a set of two blues shows in my hometown of Nancy in France—including Son Seals, Buddy Guy and Junior Wells, and Otis Rush—and B. B. King was the headliner. I was supposed to fly back home myself for the event, but was stuck in London due to a strike of air traffic controllers. I remember going to bed early and dinnerless that night in my Heathrow hotel, brooding over the fact that I had missed the chance of my life to meet my hero.

But it seems like there's more than one chance in life; back in the United States, I finally got to meet B. B. a few months later at a concert in Indiana where my friend (and then bandleader) Son Seals was appearing, and I was at last able to talk to him—and have a close look at Lucille! Over the years, several similar opportunities turned up, but it wasn't until 1982 that I recorded a formal interview with King for the first time.

Ten years later, I felt I had gathered enough material for a book and sat down to write it when a French publisher, Philippe Fréchet at Éditions du Limon, expressed his interest. It was only when the initial French version of the present work had seen the light of day that Alan Balfour in England urged me to submit my manuscript to English and American publishers. Needless to say, Alan is really the one to thank for this book, along with Chris Smith, who translated my revised manuscript into English once University Press of Mississippi had accepted it. I wish to express here my gratitude to Chris for the wonderful job he has done and the relevance of his remarks, as well as for generously sharing with me his knowledge of the blues and its history.

Others I want to thank are Jacques Périn, Jean-Pierre Arniac, Joël Dufour, André Fonteyne and Gérard Herzhaft of *Soul Bag* magazine; Dick Shurman, for his help and even more for his indefectible friendship; Gretchen Kottkamp of the Park Ridge, Illinois, Public Library for the press cuttings she sent me; David Nelson, editor of *Living Blues* magazine; and David Evans, who painstakingly edited this work with both resoluteness and humor.

Last on my list, but far from least, is JoAnne Prichard, executive editor at the University Press of Mississippi, who believed in this project from the very beginning; as my "special correspondent" she was very helpful in gathering information in her hometown of Indianola. Her patience, kindness and sense of diplomacy have been invaluable.

As B. B. King once sang, "Please Accept My Love."

INTRODUCTION

Someone wanting to sing B. B. King's praises today would probably draw up an account such as the following:

"In a career that spans half a century, B. B. King has worn out sixteen guitars making nearly fifteen thousand appearances for audiences of all races and nationalities in fifty-seven different countries, including some fifty performances for prisoners; he has recorded about seventy albums as a name artist; he has worked in cinema, television, and radio; he has written books. Since 1951, seventy-five of his songs have appeared in the *Billboard* R&B hit parades, for a total of 560 weeks (nearly eleven years!); he has won seven Grammy Awards, and, in 1987, the same year he was inducted into the Rock and Roll Hall of Fame, he was given a special Lifetime Achievement Award by the National Academy of Recording Arts and Sciences. He has also received a National Heritage Fellowship (in 1991), the Medal of the Arts from the president of the United States, and four honorary doctorates awarded by the most prestigious American universities, including Yale and the Berklee College of Music. His star is on the famous Hollywood Walk of Fame. He has fifteen children (all born out of wedlock) and two dozen grandchildren and great-grandchildren."

This is an eye-catching, if laconic, summary of an admirable and most unusual career. In some ways, B. B. King's life has conformed to one possible image of the typical blues singer: early years of poverty and hardship in the southern United States, against a backdrop of cottonfields and the muddy waters of the Mississippi River, an important musical apprenticeship in a big city—in his case, Memphis, Tennessee—and a career that has reached its peak under the spotlights of Las Vegas, amidst the sequins and the spangles. All this is true, but only in part, for it is too simplistic an account. B. B. King's real story is a great deal richer.

Riley B. King has never let up in his fight to become the living personification of the best of the blues for the whole world. In doing this, he has had several major advantages. First and most important is his above-average intelligence. Everyone who is close to him confirms that he is a very smart man, who can adapt easily to the constant change which is the very nature of show business: his music, born in the days of swing and big bands, has blossomed and made its presence felt, even as rhythm and blues, rock 'n' roll, soul, funk and rap have taken it in turn to become the height of fashion.

B. B. King's successful career is also the result of an uncommon doggedness, of paying constant attention both to what's fashionable and to wider cultural developments, and of respect for his audiences and his roots. It stands as a lesson in how to succeed, given by a brilliant man who has understood that long-term success requires sustained effort and a permanent willingness to learn. In fifty years, the man nicknamed "King of the Blues" (a title he is not very fond of) has never stopped learning and progressing, believing as he does that "to stand still is to go backwards."

He follows this basic mental discipline in his daily life as well as in music. Works on harmony and the Schillinger system of composition are usually on his bedside table during his never-ending tours (along with the instruction manual for the clarinet course which he decided to take a few years back, to improve his guitar phrasing), but B. B. King is also unable to pass a bookshop without buying a handbook on ecology or the industrial revolution, a popularizing book about computers, or a course of ten lessons on bookkeeping. As he told the sociologist Charles Keil in the early sixties, "The ninth grade was as far as I ever got in school—started the tenth grade and quit. I've always regretted that, at least since my DJ days, I've missed the lack of education. I keep taking correspondence courses on this and that, read when I get the chance. . . . Man, people think the average blues singer is stupid, and I'd like to get that out of their heads, set things straight.

" . . . I like to think I'm open to all kinds of music. You should listen to everything, take each man as he comes. I've got about fifteen thousand records in a collection at home, cylinders, lots of 78s of the older singers, and a lot of things besides blues, little bit of everything. Spanish music I like, and there's a Japanese instrument that sounds something like a guitar that knocks me out."[1]

Intelligence fires an individual's curiosity, but, in the case of B. B. King, it also emerges in the form of modesty and genuine kindness, two qualities that are almost a handicap in trying to draw an honest portrait of this artist. To make the subject's virtues credible, a biographer needs him or her occasionally to display a few faults, for contrast. Panegyric is usually unconvincing to the objective, realistic reader, but B. B. King's modesty and kindness are real; no matter how hard one looks at his past and his everyday activities, except for the fact that B. B. is a self-confessed compulsive gambler, a poor businessman and a workaholic, one would search in vain for the peccadilloes that tarnish the lives of most of us. From what has been said and written about him, it must be concluded that B. B. King's actions are motivated by a constant desire for justice and fairness. In all the testimony of admirers and friends over the last forty-five years, it is rare to find anyone expressing the slightest resentment.

In my own case, blues music had such an appeal that I left my native Europe for a time during the second half of the seventies in order to work with African-American musicians, in Chicago and on the road. For someone as much in love with R&B as I was, B. B. King was an idol, and I was lucky enough to be able to see him perform many times, and even to approach him on various occasions. Over the years, several meetings and conversations with him have shown me that the good qualities everyone recognizes in B. B. are indeed there. An exceptionally gracious host, King is unwilling to fawn. He readily answers questions for interviewers, but doesn't hesitate to test them out. Anyone who has seen him sending up an ill-informed and bumptious journalist will understand that King expects to find his own competence and honesty in others. B. B. is understanding and generous towards the many people who ask for his help; in general, he responds favorably to all reasonable requests, but does not hesitate to refuse those that are unacceptable. B. B. King likes to say yes, but he knows how to say no.

In his dressing room, at the stage door, or at social events, it is common for someone to compliment him effusively. At such times, it's striking to observe him shutting up like a clam, and it is obvious that he is genuinely shy. More than anything, King hates bragging, but he hates gushing praise, too. "If people tell me I'm a good artist, I appreciate it. To say myself that I'm great, that I can do this, or that I can move the people—I've never had that kind of confidence. . . . Sometimes, when I'm going out for a walk with a friend, he may meet someone he knows and say, 'Say, man, this is B. B. King.' I don't have the word to use for it, but it can make me feel real little, because maybe this guy he's introducing me to has never heard of B. B. King. I remember one time a guy introduced me to some girls, because he wanted to stop and chaff with them. I was just beginning to get popular then. 'Hey!' he said, all excited, 'I want you to meet B. B. King.' One of the girls asked, 'Who is B. B. King?' I could have gone through the floor, and that has stayed with me all these years. I really shiver when anyone introduces me in that way."[2]

This is the man whose story I have tried to tell here. I have been the more keen to do so because that story has rarely been written about in depth or from all angles. There are plenty of articles about B. B.'s early years, his days as a disc jockey in Memphis, even his tours with the Rolling Stones or U2, but too often the rest is forgotten. As for his authorized biography by Charles Sawyer,[3] published in 1980 and a very fine piece of work in many respects, it unfortunately downplays the discographical aspects of his career, and only discusses his music incidentally.

I felt it necessary to make good these deficiencies by trying to describe the impact that his life and his decisions have had on today's music scene. This work was first published in France, my native country, in 1993; the present version has been revised, expanded, and updated.

The publication in 1996 of B. B. King's autobiography, *Blues All Around Me*,[4] actually didn't make my own work obsolete or redundant; that book is a very moving and sincere narrative of his life and deeds, but, in many ways, it only reflects his own vision of the past. It is often very personal, and its main quality is that it includes stories and anecdotes no one else could have been expected to tell. But while King's is a book of memories, strongly focused on his childhood and the early years of his career, the present work has a much more global ambition. By exploring all aspects of King's life and career (including those that were ignored in his autobiography), it aims to provide an objective story of a man and his music, placed in proper historical perspective, with due emphasis on the observations and accounts of key witnesses. In order to accomplish this goal, I have, of course, drawn on printed sources, many of them taken from the specialized press; King's own words are also very much present, by way of the numerous interviews he has given over the years. Yet since accounts were sometimes contradictory, I have also relied on a number of encounters, from 1977 onwards, with B. B. King and Sid Seidenberg, his manager since 1968. I thank them both for their patience and understanding.

The present work is the result of this long labor of love, carried out over the course of nearly twenty years. It is my hope that readers of this book will find in it the life story of a creative genius who is also a just man.

'BLUES BOY'

1

INDIANOLA, MISSISSIPPI, SEEDS (1925-1946)

Every year since the late sixties, Riley B. King has made a musical pilgrimage through the backroads blues sheds of his native Mississippi, in memory of his friend, civil rights leader Medgar Evers, assassinated in July 1963. These "Homecoming Tours," which allow King to keep in touch with the part of the Delta where he got his start in life, invariably lead him towards Indianola, where he worked as a young man. Even though he was born on a plantation between Itta Bena and Berclair, two small towns geographically closer to Greenwood, King has always considered Indianola his hometown, even calling his album of 1970 *Indianola Mississippi Seeds*.

A few years short of the third millennium, segregation is no longer the ruling code in this rather unhurried town of ten thousand people, but whites and blacks mostly still live in clearly defined areas—even though there's been one attempt at bringing the races together in a mixed neighborhood located in the southwestern part of town. By the same token, the two communities each have their own values to celebrate, and B. B. King is not Indianola's only well-known offspring: the White Citizens' Council, one of the most virulently racist organizations in existence, was founded here in July 1954 to oppose integration in the schools.

Nowadays, his international success has made King a local star, and so his annual appearances are a chance for the Indianola town council to try to erase all traces of a dubious past. Between two "official" concerts around town, King insists on appearing for free in some of the highspots of his younger days: shabby halls in the poor neighborhoods where he hung out at the start of his career, an old club in the African-American section of Indianola, from which he gets a nostalgic charge, even Parchman Penitentiary, where his cousin Bukka White was imprisoned for two years after using violence to settle a score. It's hard to shake off twenty years of southern memories, especially for B. B. King, who proclaims his roots proudly. For him, Mississippi means his first job, his first guitar, even his first sexual experience with a lady of mature years (she was in her twenties; he was just thirteen), who destroyed many an illusion the day he offered her the five dollars he had been patiently saving for weeks.

But above all, Mississippi means Nora Ella King, his mother. Nora Ella wasn't a native of the Delta; her family came from Kilmichael, a settlement of five hundred people in the hill country to the east of the Mississippi floodplain. In the early twenties, Nora Ella and some of her relations left the country around Kilmichael to look for work in the much more fertile Delta region. Contrary to what many people believe, the Delta is not at the mouth of the Mississippi, on the Gulf of Mexico, but three hundred miles further north; the Delta, in this geographically incorrect sense, is the alluvial plain which lies between the courses of the Mississippi and Yazoo Rivers, and which extends from Memphis to Vicksburg. Over the centuries the erratic flow of these two mighty rivers has deposited layers of sediment, and the Delta has acquired some of the most fertile soil in the United States; as a result, it became the favorite landscape of King Cotton, the undisputed ruler of the local economy. At the same time—and the two facts may not be unconnected—the Delta, along with New Orleans, has been the richest center of musical development in North America.

When she and her family arrived on a plantation near Itta Bena, a village ten miles away from Greenwood, Nora Ella was not yet fifteen years old, but that didn't stop her from meeting, and very quickly marrying, Albert Lee King, a local farmworker a few years older than she. Albert King, B. B.'s father, was an orphan, and had been raised by a family named Love after being separated from his older brother Riley. From his earliest years, Albert had worked in the fields, to contribute to his adoptive family's income: it was only natural for him to want to win his independence by starting a family. After their marriage, Albert and Nora Ella King settled in a wooden cabin just west of Itta Bena to follow the only occupation open to them: working on a plantation.

In the spring of 1925, when she was barely eighteen years old, Nora Ella became pregnant, and her first child was born on 16 September. In honor of Albert's vanished brother, the baby was named Riley, with the initial "B" added—as is commonly done in the South—possibly to distinguish him from his uncle. As the man himself says, "Middle initial meaning nothing."[1] Until 1929, except for the birth of a little brother who died in infancy, life on the Itta Bena plantation followed a routine course, given its shape by the sound of the bells that announced the start of the day at dawn, six days a week. Riley was four years old when his mother suddenly left his father—a commonplace story involving two youngsters who were hardly more than twenty when they separated. Rather than staying in the Delta and risking the anger of her boss, who would be annoyed at losing her as a worker, Nora Ella decided it would be better to go back to Kilmichael, where most of her family still lived, taking her son with her. Over the next five years, Riley was raised by both Nora Ella and her own mother, Elnora Farr.

This situation was nothing unusual in a state like Mississippi, where matriarchal patterns, the heritage of slavery, were still strongly in evidence. "Much in the slave regime promoted marital and familial instability," wrote historians and sociologists August Meier and Elliott Rudwick. "Slave marriages were not recognized by law; slave sales were a frequent disrupter of family life; the miscegenation that resulted from the white males' sexual exploitation of female slaves . . . also discouraged slave married life."[2] One of the most important crusades undertaken by the African-American churches after Emancipation had been to stop the breakup of families by encouraging the newly freed to take part in traditional family structures based on white models. More than fifty years after the Civil War, though, customs born in slavery were still slow to disappear.

The head of Riley's maternal family was his great-grandfather, Pop Davidson, who had been born in slavery. B. B. King has retained a memory of his forebear as an elderly alcoholic, an authoritarian and proud man, who settled his disputes with a gun in his hand. For anyone who knows B. B. King's restrained and fundamentally benevolent nature, it's difficult to believe that he had such an ancestor. King himself is the first to recognize that he modelled his character on that of his mother, Nora Ella. Young Riley could only do this piecemeal, and for quite a short time, for he often lived with his grandmother, Elnora Farr, and, in any case, Nora Ella was soon taken from him by an illness the nature of which is uncertain. In the summer of 1935, when Riley was not yet ten years old, Nora Ella told her mother that she wanted her son to come to her at the little village of French Camp, where she was living, about fifteen miles from Kilmichael. Nora Ella became weaker, and finally called Riley to her bedside to give him her parting advice.

It is difficult for B. B. King to talk about this episode, but he has a photographic memory of it. Before she died, his mother told him to act justly and fairly in everything and at all times, without looking for anyone's approval for doing so; these principles, handed down at a time of exceptional trauma for a small boy, are the basis of B. B. King's philosophy and behavior to this day. Shortly afterwards, Nora Ella closed her eyes for the last time. Having lost his little brother, he was again confronted with death and loneliness. It's hard to say whether this experience gave him his independent nature, or if it was a natural disposition, but the fact is that King has been very private ever since.

As a result of the stresses of his childhood, he has always had a deep need for the approval of others, which made him stutter badly when he was young, and which has manifested itself in his career as a lack of confidence that is strange in an artist of his stature. As he himself says, "It's a feeling of security. When I used to play . . . you had a feeling of being liked, or loved. That was something I think I never did have quite enough of in my early years. My mother died when I was about nine and my mother and father had separated. Somehow or another I didn't have that closeness or that togetherness that I think one should have, and that left me with a little bit of a loss for love, I believe. Whenever I would sing and have these people gather around me like they did, then this seemed to me as a family. And I think that has followed me through the years."[3]

After his mother's funeral, Riley remained in Kilmichael, where he lived with his grandmother. Elnora Farr worked as a sharecropper for a family of white farmers, the Hendersons. As noted sociologist E. Franklin Frazier once put it, "sharecroppers [worked] under a system closely resembling serfdom."[4] The principle was straightforward: farmers were contracted to landowners from whom they received a wretched wooden shack and a plot of land on which they were responsible for growing and picking cotton on a crop-sharing basis. Tools and irrigation were usually provided by the landowner, but the incidental expenses, and sometimes fertilizer, were the sharecropper's responsibility. The owners of every large cotton farming operation would set up a commissary on the property, run by a trusted employee, where food, clothes and kerosene were sold to the sharecroppers on credit.

At the end of the growing season, the crop was divided between the owner and the grower, and the accounts were settled. "Dependent on lien credit for nearly all living necessities, and working under much supervision, [sharecroppers] ordinarily received no more than half the crop, from which 'furnishing' and interest was deducted," writes Paul E. Mertz in the *Encyclopedia of Southern Culture*.[5] It only took a poor harvest to make it hard for the sharecropper to repay that year's debt, and have to start over again the following year. Rather than profiting from their labors, therefore, many sharecroppers ended up financially dominated by a bossman their whole lives, unless they decided to leave. However, it must be said that in many cases, landowners were hardly better off than their tenants, especially in the hills of Mississippi, where farms were not as big as in the Delta, and crops were more meager.

Between the ages of nine and fourteen, Riley King worked for his grandmother in the fields of Edwayne Henderson. At harvest time, the least amount of labor was valuable, and children had no chance of avoiding farm work, but over the winter months, between the harvesting and the sowing seasons, the Hendersons allowed them to attend school. B. B. King's modest education took place in the single class of Elkhorn School, which survived on the generosity of the pastor and congregation of the Elkhorn Baptist Church, who sent their children there. One teacher was in charge of about a hundred children aged between six and fourteen. This man, Luther Henson, made an indelible impression on Riley King. Along with his mother's advice, Henson's teachings have been B. B. King's guiding lights all his life.

Henson had few resources with which to teach his pupils, and he set himself the objectives of teaching them to read, write and calculate; in addition he instilled in them human dignity and pride in being African-American—for how can a person who does not respect himself respect other people? In the classroom, Riley and his schoolmates were told daily about those who symbolized African-American achievement, including Louis Armstrong, Joe Louis, and Mary McLeod Bethune. Henson also wanted to inculcate a sense of self-reliance in his young pupils, by teaching them that they should support themselves throughout life, rather than looking to anyone else; for Henson, wealth consisted in spending less than one earned. This may be the area where B. B. King, an inveterate gambler, has learned his teacher's lesson least well. In all other respects, he has stayed scrupulously faithful to Henson's doctrines.

B. B. King recalls that going to school was one of his two favorite recreations, the other being music. His grandmother played no instrument, but Great-Aunt Jemimah's house held two especially precious treasures: an old harmonium and a phonograph, from which he came to know the blues. "She was one of those hip young aunts who would let me play her phonograph," King says.[6] The harmonium, or "pumping organ," as it was called, fascinated the young Riley, who enjoyed watching the grownups pedalling furiously while playing; as for the Victrola, he was allowed to use it as long as he was careful. "And that's how I got into those old blues records like Lemon Jefferson. I had a chance to fool with the organ, and that's how I learned to play a few chords."[7]

As well as these records, there was blues to be heard in the flesh, for at this time it was a natural presence in the voices of those who worked the land: "I guess the earliest sound of blues that I can remember was in the fields while people would be pickin' cotton or choppin' or somethin'. Usually one guy would be plowin' by himself or maybe one guy would take his hoe and chop way out in front of everybody else and usually you would hear this guy sing most of the time. No special lyrics or anything. Just what he felt at that time. . . . The song would be maybe somethin' like this: 'Oh I wake up in the mornin' 'bout the break of day.'

"And you could hear it just on and on like that. Also other early sounds that I used to hear was like I had an uncle called Jack Bennett and Uncle Jack would go out like early evenings to some of the games they would have, or some of the places, and on his way back home at night you would hear him sing that same kind of thing. Let's see if I can remember one: 'If I don't get home in the mornin', things are gonna be too bad.'

"And you could hear it all over the bayous. All around the many little places. And, of course, you could hear people say, 'There goes Jack . . . he's goin' home.' So I think these were a couple of the early sounds that I heard that stay with me even today. When I sing and play now I can hear those same sounds that I used to hear then as a kid. And, of course, each Monday and Wednesdays in our little neighborhood—there was nothin' else hardly to do but sing—we would go from house to house singin'. . . . And it seemed like it kept us kind of close together. That was another part of the blues that's sorta like the church social workers . . . the feeling that you get from that, especially when the kids are growing, is really togetherness."[8]

But it was gospel music, more than blues, which stimulated Riley to develop his musical talent. The great majority of African-American musicians have found their way into music through the church. King's family was no exception to this tradition: his mother and grandmother were both devoted Christians, and King's religious upbringing took place at the Elkhorn Baptist Church, or, more often, in the Holiness Church of a distant relative, Reverend Archie Fair.

Fair's doctrines were in the Pentecostal tradition, and in the eyes of his flock he was therefore a sanctified preacher. Whereas the Baptist denominations are in general more reserved in their practice of Christian ritual, the Pentecostals are well known for the exuberance of their weekly services, which go on for three or four hours. Sanctified preachers address their congregations fiercely and at length, with the aim of placing everyone in communion with the Holy Ghost. Instrumental music plays a central role throughout the service: it accompanies the singing, the dancing, and the half-chanted, half-spoken dialogues between the pastor and the faithful, until the luckiest among the latter are touched by divine grace, and fall into a trance. For some, spirit possession is manifested by fainting, while others express it by glossolalia, suddenly emitting incomprehensible sounds and words:

under the influence of the Holy Ghost, they undertake a cryptic dialogue with God in an unknown tongue.

The extremely sexual nature of these various displays of ecstasy is very striking to adult eyes. For a child the magic of such moments is unforgettable, and forever linked with the music that causes it. Riley was very much sensitized to these manifestations of the divine presence. This, more than church doctrine, was the aspect of religion that was to stay with him. Very often after the service, Reverend Fair would visit the home of William Pullian, his brother-in-law and Nora Ella's brother. Fair was playing an electric Silvertone guitar, possibly in the vehement style popularized around that time by guitar evangelist Reverend Utah Smith. While the grownups were eating, King took the opportunity to pick up Fair's guitar and try to play it. "The first electric guitar player that I heard in person though, was a sanctified preacher named Archie Fair in the hills of Mississippi. . . . When it was time for the adults to go in the kitchen for dinner (the kiddies ate later, if we were lucky), he'd lay his guitar on the bed and I'd crawl up and play with it. One day he caught me and decided to show me a few chords—C, F, and G. Even today I still use those same chords a lot, and use that I-IV-V progression in many of my songs."[9]

For a very long time, it had been Riley's dream to have his own guitar—an impossible dream for the child of a family as poor as his was. In the absence of an instrument, however, music could also be made with the voice. As a result of attending the unbridled services in Reverend Fair's Holiness Church, Riley knew he could sing, and religion supplied him with a ready-made repertoire. In those days, decidedly secular discs by the likes of Lonnie Johnson or Blind Lemon Jefferson could be found in the homes of people of his aunt's generation, but a pious family like King's was more likely to own recordings by vocal groups like the Golden Gate Quartet or the Southernaires. Together with a cousin named Birkett Davis and two school friends, Walter Doris, Jr., and Dubois Hune, Riley decided to create his first gospel group, the Elkhorn Jubilee Singers, inspired by the arrangements of his favorite groups.

Until he was fourteen, King followed his three lines of activity—school, field work, and singing. But on 15 January 1940 his grandmother died, probably of tuberculosis, and he was deprived of the only person whose affection could compensate for the loss of his mother. Initially, the Henderson family was prepared to let him continue working Elnora Farr's land, but the following autumn, after the harvest, Riley's father came to Kilmichael to pick up his son. When his first wife left him, Albert King had stayed in Mississippi, but he had remarried and was living with his new family in Lexington, a bigger town in the hills on the edge of the Delta a few miles from Highway 51, the famous road that links the South to Illinois.

After a few months in Lexington, King realized that he didn't belong there, even though he had come to like his stepmother, his three sisters and his little brother. He had left many of his memories and all his friends behind in the Mississippi hills, and he decided to go back there, cycling the sixty miles between Lexington and Kilmichael. His first impulse was to seek out the Hendersons, who entrusted him to their uncle, Flake Cartledge. Thus in the space of a few days, he not only regained both his gospel group and Elkhorn School, but also acquired an adoptive family. If Luther Henson has remained B. B. King's model of intelligence, Flake Cartledge has symbolized justice and generosity, and perhaps also fatherhood. According to King, Cartledge was a deeply religious man, who believed sincerely in the equality of all individuals, without regard to race. This was an exceptional attitude in Mississippi during the forties, a time and place where, although in theory everyone was born free and with equal rights, in reality it was not so.

Outside school hours, Riley worked on the Cartledge family's farm. The days were long, but life there had a serenity that he still misses today. To attend school, he had to walk five miles morning and evening, and his days were longer than that. In the morning before he left, and after he got back in the evening, he had ten cows to milk. "These people I worked for didn't have much money," King remembers, "but I got about fifteen dollars a month. Now, believe me, it was one of the happiest parts of my life, because there, then, they were just simple people."[10]

He also drew satisfaction from the possibility of finally making his dream a reality and buying a guitar, now that he was being paid for his work by the Cartledges. A friend of his employer's wanted to sell his guitar, and King asked his boss to buy it for him, and take the money from his wages by installments. He has remembered this instrument—a red Stella with a resonator hole—all his life.

Until it was stolen a few months later, this guitar changed Riley's daily life abruptly; for the first time ever, he actually owned something. But to own the guitar in the fullest sense meant being able to play it. After a few months, he had thoroughly mastered the three basic chords which are the very foundation of blues and gospel, and could provide efficient accompaniment for the vocal group he had formed with his cousin Birkett Davis. The latter soon left the Kilmichael area to find work in the Delta, but that didn't stop King from singing. On the other hand, the regular news that came from his cousin Birkett seemed to indicate that the Delta was livelier, and that there was a good chance of making a living there.

During the spring of 1943, Riley persuaded his cousin to drive over and find him; he said goodbye to the Cartledge family, collected his guitar and his few belongings together, and left his mother's birthplace for good. War was raging in the Pacific and in Europe, and there was a labor shortage; as a result he immediately found employment as a farmworker on Johnson Barrett's plantation, only eight miles away from Indianola. As was normal in a region as fertile as the Delta, the Barrett plantation was much more extensive than the Hendersons' or the Cartledges' modest farms in the Kilmichael hills; it was also more modern, since Barrett owned several tractors at a time when most farms were still cultivated with mules. Strictly speaking, Barrett wasn't a major landowner, for he didn't own the thousand acres he farmed, but his business still provided a living for some fifty sharecroppers and their families—including King and his cousin Birkett. From the outset, Riley King proved himself to be intelligent and competent; after spending some time behind one of his employer's mules, he was finally entrusted with one of the tractors. Instead of doing manual work, King was valued for his skills, and this was reflected in his pay. In the early 1940s most cotton pickers were paid between fifty cents and a dollar per hundred pounds; a daily crop of three hundred pounds was not unusual, and some did pick as many as five hundred pounds a day, which is what, King says in his autobiography, he and his cousin could pick. Yet a good tractor driver would make up to five dollars a day in much less tiring conditions.

Given the international situation, however, this state of affairs could not last. On 16 September 1943, his eighteenth birthday, King was obliged to report to the draft board to set matters straight with the military. A few months later, he was summoned for basic training to Camp Shelby, in Hattiesburg, Mississippi, where he spent three months. But he was not sent to fight; his status as a tractor driver—"I was one of the top tractor drivers," he boasts even today—meant that he was able to fulfil his service obligations by working for his boss, Johnson Barrett, thanks to an agreement with the army whereby the big plantation owners sold part of their output to the military authorities.

Even though Riley King's employment was on the Barrett plantation, he was a conscript, which meant that he could not leave, at least before the war ended. This might have remained a minor irritation, had not the presence of German prisoners of war, hired out as day labor to planters in Sunflower County, awakened him to a sense of racial injustice. The POWs were contracted to pick only two hundred pounds of cotton per day; also, the plantation's African-American workers would have already been working in the fields for a long time when the Germans were brought along by their guards, and the prisoners' working day ended sooner than that of the black laborers. "This got to me sometimes. It wasn't that I thought the POWs should be treated more harshly, but the fact that we led a harder life than captured enemy soldiers seemed unfair to me."[11]

Even though his fate was in the hands of the U. S. Army, nothing in Riley King's way of life had really changed. In particular, there was nothing to stop him leading the same social life as his friends on Saturday nights and Sundays. Like them, he enjoyed heading for the clubs in Indianola to listen to music, especially with his sweetheart, Martha Denton, who had become by then the first Mrs. King.

Riley and his young wife lived with Martha's brother, but they often socialized with Birket Davis, with whom King had started a new gospel group as soon as he got to Indianola. Other members were N. C. Taylor, Nathaniel Parker and O. L. Matthews, under the leadership of the latter's brother, John Matthews, who had christened the group the Famous St. John Gospel Singers. Like many religious quartets of the kind, they sang all over the Delta at the invitation of the many local African-American congregations. In order to be more widely known, they had even managed to appear on some local radio stations.

Until the end of the forties, few stations in the United States bothered about African-American listeners; this was less a matter of racism than of purely economic considerations, for sponsors were reluctant to support broadcasts aimed at an audience that owned comparatively few receivers per head, had little discretionary cash to buy advertisers' products, and did much of their shopping at the plantation commissary. For reasons mostly connected with America's puritanical outlook, the first experiments in programming for African-American audiences leaned on religious music, which was thought more worthy of the airwaves than the dubious songs of wandering blues singers. In Mississippi, the managers of WGRM in Greenwood and WGVM in Greenville were among the rare pioneers in this field. The set-up suited them, insofar as the quartets were happy to sing for nothing if they could announce the details of their upcoming appearances over the air. So it was that the Famous St. John Gospel Singers became regulars at the studios of WGRM and WGVM, a fact which never ceased to amaze their guitar player, Riley King. "It was something different. I had never been on the radio, in fact I didn't really know what radio was about. A little bit unbelievable to go and see this one microphone sitting there, and then we sing and some little box some place could pick it up. I couldn't understand that!"[12]

If the Delta radio stations which allotted a few hours each week to the African-American population generally limited themselves to gospel music, one station was about to become famous by programming blues musicians. This trailblazer was KFFA, which broadcast from Helena, a town in Arkansas, on the west bank of the Mississippi. KFFA had been founded in 1941, a few days before the United States went to war, and was the brainchild of Sam W. Anderson, a former head teacher who had gone into business. As a shrewd businessman, Anderson looked for sponsors among local companies; one of the first to show an interest in his station was Max Moore, whose firm marketed cornmeal, a basic ingredient of southern African-American cooking.

Not long before, W. Lee "Pappy" O'Daniel, one of Moore's rivals in the cornmeal business, had become famous in Texas by sponsoring a western swing broadcast; it had been so successful that it not only increased his sales considerably, but propelled him into the office of state governor after an election upset. When two blues singers from around Helena, Rice Miller—calling himself Sonny Boy Williamson—and Robert Junior Lockwood, turned up at the KFFA studios one morning in December 1941, Anderson and Moore, inspired by O'Daniel's example, realized that they could make good use of a blues program presented by local musicians, and boosting the merits of King Biscuit flour.

In a few weeks, it seemed as though the entire African-American population of the Delta was getting together every day at noon to listen to Sonny Boy and Robert Junior on KFFA, and sales of King Biscuit flour were booming beyond all expectations: *King Biscuit Time* was on its way to attaining legendary status. Sonny Boy Williamson died in 1965 after having become internationally renowned, but to this day KFFA still plays his records every day at the same hour.

It's no exaggeration to say that *King Biscuit Time* had a great influence on the postwar blues scene in the Delta, as much because of its audience as because of the performing careers it supported. Apart from the many musicians who backed Sonny Boy on the air, a surprising number of famous musicians, from Muddy Waters to Howlin' Wolf and Elmore James, were faithful listeners. Among their number was B. B. King. "Oh yes! I used to listen to Sonny Boy and them all the time. That was one of our inspirations. You didn't have any other live blues music that was like *King Biscuit Time*. The late Rice Miller. When *King Biscuit Time* was on, everybody stopped working in the fields to listen to them. We would have missed them for nothing in the world!"[13]

Blues might be rarely heard on the radio, but it was there in most of the black bars, clubs and taverns scattered across the Delta. On Saturday night, everybody went out to Johnny Jones's in Indianola, Horace Bloomfield's in Marks, or the Green Spot and the Brick Yard in Clarksdale, some of the many juke joints, those ramshackle cafes where nationally known acts appeared alongside anonymous local ones. Sometimes Riley and Martha were able to go into Indianola to see one of their idols. Johnny Jones, the owner of Jones' Night Spot on Church Street, put on topflight presentations; not only did local artists like Robert Nighthawk, Sonny Boy and Robert Junior appear there, but also Louis Jordan and his Tympany Five and the big bands of Jay McShann, Count Basie and even Duke Ellington. But although the youngsters would see posters announcing these shows, they were short of money, and travel was difficult. If you didn't know someone with a car, it was a matter of walking the eight miles between the plantation and Indianola, and having very sore feet when it was time to dance.

At first, Riley King wasn't very interested in blues, preferring to concentrate on the activities of his gospel group, but one after another the quartet members had their worlds changed by the arrival of children, and found that music was taking second place to family life. Riley and Martha had no children, and King was thinking more and more seriously about music. Even as he was becoming somewhat skeptical about religion, so the blues was becoming uppermost in his thoughts, especially after his stay at Camp Shelby: "I was listening to the blues from the time I guess I was seven or eight years old. But I didn't really start trying to play the blues until I was old enough to go into the service."[14]

Another element in this process of change was the sudden realization by the singer that his guitar could do more than simply accompany. With the guitar, one could prolong the song, develop it and embellish it. Whereas King had been satisfied up to now with the three basic chords that Reverend Fair had taught him some years previously, his approach to his instrument was about to be revolutionized by the discovery of two important guitarists whose influence is at the root of what later became B. B. King's style. During his military hitch, thanks to a buddy named Willie Dotson, he discovered Django Reinhardt. Dotson was serving in France, and when he was on leave in 1944 he brought back some 78 rpm discs by the jazz musician. "My friend brought back with him several recordings of the Hot Club of France. That's how I became familiar with Django, and it was about the same time that I discovered Charlie Christian."[15]

The melodic romanticism of the French jazz musician and the dexterity of Benny Goodman's guitarist might seem a long way from the blues as it was played in the Delta during the forties, but the single-note work of these two great innovators had already given King an inkling of all the remarkable things he would eventually do with his guitar. Along with Sam McCrary, the impassioned lead singer of a gospel quartet named the Fairfield Four, Christian and Reinhardt were the chief heroes in B. B. King's personal hall of fame, and the forces at work in a slow process of change that was to make Riley King, model tractor driver and gospel singer of conviction, a creative force in the blues.

It seems to have come as a revelation when he realized that the success he had always enjoyed while appearing in church could be much greater, and much more lucrative, if gospel gave way to blues, and if the fervor of Pentecostal congregations was replaced by the enthusiasm of a street audience. One Saturday afternoon when the other members of the Famous St. John Gospel Singers were unavailable, King decided to work solo with his guitar on the streets of Indianola. When he came home that evening, he had twice the money in tips that he had made from a week's work on the Barrett plantation, and his mind was made up: the blues could open doors that so far had only been pushed ajar in his imagination. Not wanting people in Indianola to become tired of him, Riley spent some of his pay on travel during the succeeding weeks, and played in each of the main towns nearby. In Greenville, in Greenwood, and in Marks, his street performances were met with enthusiasm.

"In Indianola, [I played] on the corner of Church and Second Street. Second Street is like the main part of town, and Church Street crossed it and went into the black area, what we called 'across the tracks.' I never passed the hat, but the people knew that I'd appreciate a dime if I played a tune they'd requested.

" . . . On my corner both the blacks and the whites would see me. It wasn't something I planned; it was just like a good fishing place—it seemed like a nice spot to be. You'd find me on that corner on Saturdays, and sometimes after I got off work I'd take my bath, get my guitar, and hitchhike to other little towns like Itta Bena or Moorhead or Greenville. Most times I was lucky. I'd make more money that evening than I'd make all week driving tractors. I'd probably have enough money for a movie. Next day, go to church, then back to work."[16]

After a few months of this routine, King's thoughts were centered more and more on his guitar and less and less on his tractor. The end of the war came in the summer of 1945, and, with it, his obligation to stay on the Barrett plantation. He wasn't worried by the idea of leaving. "Every autumn, after our crops was gathered, I would say, 'Hey, now is the time to go,' and we'd make plans to leave and go to Memphis or someplace where we could record. But every time that would happen, they'd say, 'No. We didn't do too well . . . so we won't do it.' . . . Everybody was very conscious of their families, which I can understand. But I guess I wasn't as family-oriented as they were. I kept thinking that we could go off and do like the Golden Gate Quartet and many of the other groups."[17] After experiencing Indianola, Lexington and Kilmichael, he was certain that Mississippi held no great opportunities for him. He had plenty of destinations to choose from. A few of his contemporaries had headed south for New Orleans, but the vast majority of those who decided to abandon what little the Delta offered to find a better life elsewhere chose to travel up Highway 49 towards Memphis, St. Louis and Chicago.

The only reason Riley might have had to hesitate was his wife, Martha, who yearned for a peaceful and stable existence rather than the terrors of the unknown and an uncertain future. King needed an excuse to make a decision. It came in May 1946. "This particular evening, boy, I'd been flyin' all day, man, and everything was cool. I'm thinking about a lady I'm going to go see that night, ran the tractor up like we usually do, cut it off, get off there, and that sucker turned over a few times more. And when it did, under the house it went! That broke off the exhaust. Scared me so bad—I knew my boss was going to have a fit! . . . I left . . . that night."[18]

Panic-stricken at the thought of his responsibility for this accident, King rushed home; without stopping to ask for his week's pay, he picked up his guitar and left the Barrett plantation in a hurry, without even telling Martha. Before the sun had set, Riley was moving along the highway towards Memphis, his only luggage his instrument and the princely sum of two dollars and fifty cents.

2
RADIO DAYS (1947-1951)

In April 1991, Willie W. Herenton surprised everyone by becoming the first African-American mayor of Memphis, a city still afflicted by the casual, paternalist racism which has long governed relations between its communities. Although 55 percent of the population of America's fifteenth-largest city is black, until the 1990s the weight of custom in the conservative Old South, lingering fears from the days of segregation, and apathy in an electorate ill prepared for the complexities of American democracy had stood in the way of such a development.

Today's city seems light-years away from the time when prominent members of the Irish and Italian communities ran its underworld with an iron hand in a velvet glove. During the first years of the century, Herenton's most famous predecessor, Edward H. Crump, had campaigned on a platform of closing the brothels that were flourishing in the red-light districts; after his election in 1909, he found it was more realistic to try to keep them under control. As a consequence, gambling and prostitution remained very much alive in the Beale Street neighborhood until its decline at the end of the 1960s due to urban renewal.

It would be wrong and simplistic, however, to blame the local politicos for all the city's problems. It was always a wide-open town, but geography was the main reason. Memphis lies on the Mississippi, halfway between New Orleans and the big cities of the Midwest, and, since the early nineteenth century, it had been a way station for all kinds of adventurers as they sought their fortunes in the little-known lands to the north and west. Important as both a center of rail traffic and a river port, as well as being the acknowledged capital of the cotton industry, Memphis quickly became a crossroads of humanity.

The liveliest part of town was Beale Street. It had been named in the 1840s, but today nobody seems to know whether the Beale so honored was Edward or George, and whether he was a general or a captain. At its western end, Beale meets the banks of the Mississippi, where there used to be hordes of longshoremen and porters of all races. The eastern end of Beale, on the other hand, once was a desirable residential district. But the most colorful part of this urban artery runs from Main Street to the intersection with Danny Thomas Boulevard (once Wellington Street). At one time, in the space of a few hundred yards, one could find various gambling dens and dives alongside nicer clubs, theatres and restaurants, as well as the storefronts of hardware dealers, pawn brokers, lawyers, doctors, dentists and sanctified preachers, as in any business and entertainment district.

At the turn of the century, the hottest of Beale's joints was Pee Wee's, a notorious saloon run by an Italian named Maffei. "A popular joke at his bar was 'We can't close yet, no one has been killed,'" reported Memphis blues specialist Bengt Olsson.[1] Other such landmarks of culture and etiquette included the Midway Café, whose owners invariably seemed to die violently, and the Monarch, nicknamed "the castle of missing men" because there was a patch of rough ground between the back of it and the local funeral parlor; when the Monarch's bouncers, Cousin Hog and Bad Sam, tossed out the bodies of murdered customers, it was a simple matter for the undertaker's assistants to pick them up. So goes the legend.

From the twenties on, the African-American population of Memphis grew rapidly with the arrival of migrants from the Delta, and Beale Street became its favorite meeting place. The likes of the Ashford Saloon and Jim Mulcahy's place gave way to a row of clubs and theaters: the Club Handy, the Lincoln, the Old Daisy and the New Daisy, but above all the Palace, the street's most famous black establishment. With the exception of special "Midnight Ramble" shows, white patrons were not admitted to the Palace, where it was amateur night every Tuesday in the late thirties. For those musicians who missed winning a prize, there was still a chance to play for the public a short distance away, in Handy Park, an unlikely patch of green in the heart of the city. Along with alcohol, women, and gambling, the common denominator of all these places was, of course, the blues.

Nowadays, Memphis has chosen to capitalize on the nostalgia of its visitors who have kept fond memories of the early days of soul music and rock 'n' roll. Lovers of the solid, brassy sound of the Stax label can see the vacant lot on McLemore Avenue where the firm's building once stood, and artists from all over the world insist on recording in the city's mythic R&B nests—Ardent Studio or Willie Mitchell's Royal Studio—after attending a Sunday service at the church of repentant soul star Reverend Al Green. Rock 'n' roll, said to have been born here, is content to pull in pilgrims from all over the world to Graceland, the cathedral of kitsch that was once Elvis Presley's home. After eagerly inspecting the King's jungle and trophy rooms, tourists walk across Elvis Presley Boulevard to the many souvenir stores located next to Presley's private jet planes, where they can buy curtains carrying his portrait, or visit one of the so-called museums there and take a snapshot of the first television he shot at point-blank range because the bad guy in a Western was giving the hero a hard time.

As for the blues, the very root of rock 'n' roll, these days it seems confined to being presented in typical boogie clubs for mostly white tourists following the nostalgia trail. Too often, these clubs prefer booking the standard touring blues acts; consequently, much of the city's indigenous black talent isn't given a chance to perform on Beale Street at all. This is all the more regrettable as Memphis still has a vibrant and quite varied musical scene today; much of the best of it is poorly supported and remains underground, while a lot of generic music is offered for tourists.

Things were very different just after the war, when blues was the cultural expression of the African-American underclass, and popular only with those whose outlet it was. In the twenties, the blues in Memphis was shaped by musicians like Frank Stokes, Furry Lewis and Jim Jackson. Street singers, storytellers, and medicine show entertainers, these pioneer artists dominated the local scene along with the jug bands. With a lineup usually of guitar, kazoo, harmonica and jug—an earthenware pitcher, used to imitate a tuba—the likes of Will Shade's Memphis Jug Band and Gus Cannon's Jug Stompers performed popular songs for their roaring twenties audiences. Although these bands survived into the 1960s, they were in serious decline by the Second World War, as the raw blues sounds of the Delta appeared on Beale Street along with a mass influx of Mississippi and Arkansas farmworkers, drawn by the job opportunities offered by defense work. This was the Memphis that presented itself to a farmboy named Riley King in the spring of 1946.

"They often say that you can take the boy out of the country, but you can't get the country out of the boy. So when I first left I was hitchhiking and I ran across a guy with a truck. He had what we call a transport truck and he was distributin' flour," B. B. King remembered in a *Living Blues* interview. "I asked him if he'd let me ride with him to Memphis, I'd help him unload his flour. He said, 'Yeah.' I had walked about fifteen, twenty miles when I saw this guy. He passed by me at the store. I started to help him unload his flour and I got into Memphis about 3:30 in the mornin'. I didn't have any money but this guy had fed me gittin' me to Memphis. He had food with him in his truck. . . . So he took me to the Union Station in Memphis and that's where I sit until the next morning.

" . . . That was the very first time I went to Memphis. And Memphis was to me as large as I'd ever saw. I was really like a kid in a candy store. I started lookin' at the big buildings and seein' how the people lived there. I saw streetcars for the first time. I had a chance to get up close to trains . . . I saw all of these big locomotives and boy, these very long trains and people ridin' on 'em. And all of this was new to me. And they told me that at this station people could leave and go to Chicago, New York, or California . . . It was really fun for me."[2]

Once he had got over these surprises, Riley King's first thought was to find the only relative he knew of in Memphis, a cousin on his mother's side named Bukka White. Without an address, he naturally started looking at the focal point of the black community, the famous Beale Street, which he'd always heard spoken of as the home of the blues. Since he wanted to make a living as a blues singer, Beale Street was an obvious place to go. Unable to afford a hotel room, he walked to Union Station and spent his first night in an old railroad car and the next stretched out on a bench in an all-night gambling joint on Beale. After two days, his patience was rewarded, and he found his cousin in the neighborhood called Orange Mound.

Over the next few months, King enjoyed Bukka White's hospitality. White even got his cousin a job at the place where he worked. "He was working over at Lauderdale and Vance at a place called Newberry Equipment Company. He got me a job working with him. We used to make tanks that they used in service stations. . . . These big transfer trucks that carry fuel from place to place—we made those, too."[3]

King had a clear memory of Bukka White from his childhood; Bukka's fierce guitar playing had impressed him, as had the convincing way he worked his personal experiences into his music. Above all, though, he had been struck by the way Bukka held the guitar flat across his knees to play a song called "Poor Boy," and slid a metal tube along the frets, somewhat in the way that Hawaiian guitarists played. Before the war, Booker T. Washington White had been one of the most original blues musicians in Mississippi, and his extremely forceful style had even attracted record company talent scouts. In late 1937, however, his career as a recording artist was interrupted by a run-in with the law, as a result of which he spent two years wearing stripes in Parchman Penitentiary.

White had a real influence on King's career, as has often been pointed out. He himself claimed that he had influenced the career path of the man he affectionately called "Cousin B" by giving him his first guitar when he was six, but this tale has never been confirmed by its subject, and is probably apocryphal. Nevertheless, it seems likely that White, who was King's senior by sixteen years, helped his young cousin when he arrived in Memphis, most notably through buying him a Gibson guitar and an amplifier in the O.K. Houck Music Store downtown. "When B come here to get him a job and start playing music, his daddy told me I was a damned fool for going out there and spending for that stuff because B wasn't going to pay for it. Well, I said, I could see the good in it," Bukka remembered later.[4]

Whatever the truth of the matter, if Riley admired White's music, he was even more impressed by the older man's charisma and whimsical personality. "He influenced me from the time I was a little boy—as a person, not really as a musician. . . . I did not take any repertoire from Bukka. Not only was he my cousin, but he had the kind of personality that made me want to laugh. . . . When we were kids, he'd always come by with candy, and if there was an argument he could always straighten it out without nobody being angry. . . . But his playing did not influence me, with the exception of my trying to imitate his bottleneck sound. We were in two different worlds."[5]

It was Beale Street more than Bukka White that inspired King. After the first excitement of novelty, he was at once overwhelmed by the variety of sounds available and downcast by the realization that the blues scene was managing very well without him. Everywhere he went, on every corner and in all the bars on the street, he heard guitarists and singers who were as good as he was. "Beale Street isn't what it used to be," he explained to producer and journalist Pete Welding a few years ago, "and it was really Beale *Avenue*, not Beale Street. It's about a quarter-mile long, ten or twelve blocks, from the river to the east. I remember when Handy's Park used to be like a circus. Beale Street runs along its south side, Third Street on the west, and Hernando on the east. There used to be parties, jug bands, and everything going on there. Something in each corner but the crowd usually ended up with the blues singers. It wasn't like a theater with the names up outside. There you had to be heard, and whenever a fellow got to feeling good, there all the people would go. But it got to be so noisy that the all-white police ran the cats out. They were attracting so much attention that they were tying up traffic on Third Street, which is a main thoroughfare."[6]

In Memphis, the blues was played in the streets but also in the various establishments along Beale Street, where the most assertive singers and instrumentalists competed for the best-paying jobs. One of the leading places for music was Sunbeam Mitchell's Club Handy, where the best traveling musicians coming through Memphis would usually stay, since Mitchell also ran a hotel there. "Let's assume that we were going through town: we'd go to Mitchell's, because we'd have a chance to see the best and find out what's goin' on in the city. That's where you get your information," King remembers.[7]

One of the first black theaters on Beale Street was the Lincoln, the construction of which was financed by the local African-American community. Its success bred imitators, like the Grand Theater—later renamed the New Daisy—or the Palace, which was one of the most celebrated venues in the South by the end of the thirties. For a young unknown like Riley King, the Palace was the only place to go looking for work; it was there that Professor Nat D. Williams, a teacher and journalist well known in the community for his enterprising ways, had instituted a weekly amateur talent contest.

"When I first came to Memphis," King says, "Beale Street was very active then. Many little clubs on Beale Street, with music going on all up and down the street on the weekend, so you could find some of the best players, even guys with names would come and play or listen to people play. At that time, there was three theaters, movie picture theaters. Two of them used to have amateur shows. One was called the New Daisy Theater, and the one where it had amateur shows every Tuesday or Wednesday night was the Palace Theater. So all of the amateur musicians used to come in there because if you're able to go on the stage, you would get a dollar, and if you won you got five dollars, and everybody tried to go. Including myself, many times. Well, you found a lot of folk guitar players like [Frank] Stokes, Bukka White—my cousin—Robert Nighthawk, and of course later on Earl Hooker and all of us would go through there, even after I made records, I still would go there sometimes."[8]

By the time King came to Memphis, drummer Al Jackson was leading the house band at the Palace and Nat Williams had handed over the presenter's job to Rufus Thomas, another colorful singer and MC who had a day job in a suitcase factory. Thomas went on to be a radio announcer, and then a local rhythm and blues star who racked up a succession of dance hits on labels like Sun and Stax. He remembered his time at the Palace for the critic and author Peter Guralnick: "First they had the movies and then the amateur, which was the bottom hour, and then it was back to the movies. I reached back and got a friend of mine, his name was Robert Counts, they called him Bones, and we were together for eleven consecutive years at the Palace Theater every Wednesday night. I tell you, you wouldn't believe this, but we were making five dollars a night. . . . Course the show was only a nickel then, but the place was packed. In the beginning we used to have $5, $3, and $2 for prizes, but then they cut that out and everybody who come up on stage would get a dollar. B. B. used to come with holes in his shoes, his guitar all patched up, just to get that dollar."[9]

Riley seems not to have been lucky, however. After ten months without ever winning first prize at the Palace he was discouraged, and decided to head back to the Delta. Music wasn't the only factor in this decision. Unable to break into the local blues scene, King had had to settle for his job at the Newberry Company, and his standard of living was suffering as a result. Even if returning to Indianola meant that he wouldn't be making a living from music, he could go back to his reasonably well-paid job as a tractor driver, and his wife, Martha, was waiting there for him.

On top of that, the hasty way he had left the plantation was bothering him. "I missed my family and I missed everything. So I went back down there and told [my boss] what happened. He laughed then. I told him, 'I'm sorry, and I came back to pay for it,' which I did."[10]

Early in 1947, King went home and got his old job back. He hadn't given up the idea of becoming a famous blues singer, but he told himself that a few months of saving money would make this easier when he went back to Memphis. The decisive moment came at the end of 1948, after the cotton harvest was finished on the Barrett plantation. This time Riley left with his head high, his modest savings in his pocket, promising his wife that he would send for her as soon as he could afford to.

As it turned out, the change of fortune that he had been awaiting for so long happened more quickly than he could have hoped. Coincidence played its part in the success of this second attempt, but it is also true that this time Riley was aware of the way the music business worked in Memphis, and had every intention of using the system to his advantage. As soon as he got back to the city, he left his belongings with Bukka White and went over to West Memphis, on the west bank of the Mississippi, to meet with harmonica player Rice Miller (Sonny Boy Williamson).

Radio station KWEM in West Memphis had recently started aiming some of its programming at local African-Americans, and Sonny Boy was presenting a daily fifteen-minute show. King was well aware of Sonny Boy, having heard him many times in the Delta, on the well-known program *King Biscuit Time* over KFFA; he was surprised to hear Sonny Boy on KWEM while listening to the radio at his cousin's, and, plucking up his courage, he went to the studio, introduced himself to his idol, and asked if he could back him during his broadcasts. "I can't explain it, but . . . it seems like I had heard Sonny Boy on the radio so much that I felt like I already know him," King laughs.[11]

Sonny Boy Williamson was always famous for his craftiness, and the young guitarist's unexpected offer enabled him to get out of a tricky situation. At that time, he was appearing at the 16th Street Grill in West Memphis, a saloon where blues, dancing and cards were equally important attractions. However, he had taken a second engagement on the same day in Clarksdale, Mississippi. "One paid twelve dollars and the other, out of the city, $100 or $150. So he called the lady for whom he had been playing the twelve dollar job, a Miss Annie who owned the Sixteenth Street Grill in [West] Memphis. She had heard the program for he advertised the Grill. In fact, it was one of the functions of having your own radio program to talk up the place where you played."[12] "He said I'm going to send him down in my place tonight—he hadn't even asked me," King laughs.[13] He adds modestly, "He told me: 'You'd better play good, boy, because if you don't, you'll have to answer to me.' I'll never forget that. And that was the first time I played a professional job in the Memphis area. I liked it very much because it was my job to entertain the ladies while the fellers went in the back and played cards."[14]

It appears that Riley was successful in carrying out his instructions. After he had finished playing, Miss Annie offered him work on other nights, provided that he managed to get a regular radio show like Sonny Boy's. As an incentive, Miss Annie offered the handsome payment of twelve dollars a day, six days a week, plus board and lodging. For someone like Riley, fresh from the country, it was unthinkable to refuse such a tempting offer, and he immediately started looking for a radio station that would take him on. It wouldn't have been right to trespass on Sonny Boy Williamson's territory, so the logical place to go was WDIA in Memphis.

In 1948 there were few programs aimed at African-Americans in the United States, and especially not in a southern city like Memphis. WDIA had been launched on 7 June 1947 by two white businessmen; it had started by playing country music, without much success, and had then tried to win a different audience with a mixture of pop songs and classical music. The results were unpromising, and, faced with imminent closure, Bert Ferguson, one of the station managers, decided on a last-ditch experiment: an attempt to attract the African-American community in Memphis and the surrounding counties, who were a potential audience almost half a million strong. At the end of October 1948 he called on the services of Professor Nat D. Williams, the very man who had run the talent nights at the Palace on Beale Street for a long time. In just a few weeks, the hoped-for miracle had taken place, and black advertisers and black audiences alike had rallied to WDIA.

Like most of his community, Riley King knew about WDIA through hearing Nat D. Williams's new show, and he decided to try his luck there. Leaving West Memphis and the 16th Street Grill in the morning, he took a bus into downtown Memphis, which was as far as his money would take him, and covered the last few miles between the Greyhound terminal and WDIA's studios at 2074 Union Avenue on foot. It was pouring rain, and he had to wrap his guitar in newspaper to keep it from getting wet. By the time he got to WDIA, the army jacket he was wearing was soaked through, and he entered the building feeling that he must look like a mess and a sorry sight. Through the studio window, he could see Nat D. Williams on the air. The show had barely finished before King knocked on the door and was invited into the studio by the disc jockey, who asked what he could do for him. Summoning up all the confidence he could muster, the young man replied without batting an eyelid that he wanted to cut a record and make a broadcast.

At a station like WDIA, a decision as important as this could only be taken with the agreement of Mr. Ferguson, the manager. The prospect of recording a novice blues singer didn't interest him, but Ferguson was very keen to consolidate the station's popularity with its African-American audience. He asked the young man's name, and then invited him to play something on his guitar. King started to play Ivory Joe Hunter's hit, "Blues at Sunrise." "They'd just got a new product called Pepticon, which was going to be competition for Hadacol, a tonic that had been big. He called the program director and he said, 'We've got ten minutes open, from 3:30 to 3:40, with nothing set. Let's put him in there.' So I sang a couple of songs . . . as the Pepticon Boy."[15] An ironic twist was that, at this time, Hadacol, Pepticon's chief competitor, was sponsoring Sonny Boy Williamson on KWEM!

For the new show, King composed an advertising jingle, which he sang live every day at the start of his show: "Pepticon, Pepticon, sure is good / You can get it anywhere in your neighborhood." Every Saturday afternoon from 5:00 to 5:15, he performed two or three songs live before signing off, not forgetting to say where and when he was appearing next. King received no fee from WDIA, but he was allowed to publicize himself freely over the air, so Miss Annie's instructions were fully carried out.

King's radio debut marks the point where his career really took off. Since that day in late 1948, King has never stopped progressing, either musically or in popularity. Thanks to this unexpected piece of luck he was able to make himself known as a talented artist around Memphis, before his genius was unleashed on the rest of the world. The few short years from 1948 to 1953 when he worked at WDIA saw the blossoming of his talent, the start of his success, and the arrival of the name he is known by today, B. B. King. "The Boy from Beale Street, they would say. People started to write me quite a bit. First they would say B. B.—the blues boy; sometimes they would say, B. B.—the Beale Street Blues Boy; and then they stopped doing that and would just say Blues Boy."[16] King's close friends took the process one step further, calling him just "B."

King left the WDIA studios that first day still rather surprised at how easily he had got himself a show, and went back to Miss Annie's to tell her the good news and settle in as a lodger. Over the succeeding weeks, his life revolved around two main activities: his weekly broadcast over WDIA and his daily shows at the 16th Street Grill. The radio brought him a bigger audience at every live show, and at the same time his radio following grew as more people came to the Grill. Miss Annie was more than satisfied with his increasing success, and his pay soon rose from twelve to twenty-five dollars.

The Blues Boy wasn't idle during the week. His appearances over the air were unpaid, but he more than made up for that by taking part in promotional events organized in Memphis by the makers of Pepticon. In one neighborhood after another, the man christened "the Pepticon Boy" on these occasions would systematically visit the stores where the tonic was sold, singing and playing guitar while a salesman from Pepticon pressed bottles of the miraculous product on members of the public who would gather on the pavement. "When they would sell so many, they would usually give me a bonus for going out. Sometimes I would get fifty or sixty or maybe a hundred dollars just for being out that day, and that was very big money for me," says King.[17] He adds with a smile, "One of the salesmen said they would listen to me because they could see I had an honest face!"[18]

During this auspicious time King developed a strong enthusiasm for gambling which has never left him. Some of his money went on this new craze, and all kinds of spongers borrowed money from him, which he never saw again. But he did not let his generosity get in the way of keeping his promise to bring his wife, Martha, to Memphis.

Suddenly everything was looking good; in April of 1949 his weekly broadcasts became daily from 5:30 until 5:45 as WDIA tried to strengthen its programming to take advantage of the booming interest in radio among African-Americans. Then the management gave him a second show, every afternoon from 12:30 to 12:45; noon was an experimental hour, and B. B. became the first African-American to have a regular fifteen-minute segment at this time of day on WDIA. The Blues Boy was in the right place at the right time, thanks as much to the novelty of radio programs made by and for African-Americans as to his own talents.

For all that, his talents as a radio announcer were undeniable. As he has often admitted himself, King's command of English is less accomplished than his blues singing, and the shyness of his childhood has never quite left him, but perhaps because he spoke simply and directly, his broadcasts found favor with a working-class audience who encountered in them their own culture and the things that mattered to them. In addition, Riley, who was a self-conscious youngster in everyday life, underwent a dramatic personality change when the red light went on in the studio. Chris Spindel, the program director at WDIA in the late forties, retains a clear memory of this extraordinary transformation: "He was skinny then. He looked so sad . . . and he'd be so shy all the time."[19] But as soon as King was on the air, all trace of timidity vanished; his voice became all that mattered.

Along with his daily gigs at the 16th Street Grill, on weekends B. B. King would travel to the small towns in the tri-state area—the parts of Tennessee, Arkansas and Mississippi around Memphis. King soon realized that the customers who came to have fun in the clubs where he played on Saturday nights wanted to dance to the hits of the day, and wanted the sound of a classy orchestra rather than his lone guitar. In any case, several Memphis musicians who knew that he didn't have a band wanted to benefit from his burgeoning fame, and suggested that he should team up with them. As a result, B. B. King got to know a group of young musicians as talented and ambitious as he was himself, who were also seeking their place in the sun, men like drummers Earl Forrest and E. A. Kamp, piano players Ford Nelson and John "Ace" Alexander, and saxophonists Richard Sanders, Solomon Hardy and Herman Green. "I began to run into guys who are now very big in the jazz field," says King. "George Coleman who [later] was with Miles Davis. Herman Green, who was with Lionel Hampton, was with me for a time, and so was George Joyner, the bassist."[20]

Encountering other musicians played a decisive part in B. B. King's musical development. Hitherto, he had been content to play with feeling but without paying much attention to structure; in this respect, he was closer to the more old-fashioned musicians, like John Lee Hooker or Lightnin' Hopkins, who would add extra bars as their mood and the vagaries of improvisation suggested. Playing with accompanists ruled out this kind of freedom. Laboriously at first, he learned to conform to the rules his band imposed on him. "We worked together, but they didn't always like it, because my timing was so bad. My beat was all right—I'd keep that —but I might play 13 or 14 bars on a 12-bar blues! Counting the bars—that was out! These guys would hate that, because they had studied, but all my musical knowledge was what I'd got from records. I tried to play it right, but I ended up playing it my way. The one thing they did like was that I paid well. I could afford to pay them twenty or twenty-five dollars, and if I made more, I paid more."[21]

One of his toughest teachers was the guitarist Robert Junior Lockwood. Unlike his other friends in the music business, Lockwood was a veteran, raised in the tough school of the legendary blues singer Robert Johnson, who had lived with Lockwood's mother for a time. Robert Junior was also in at the start of *King Biscuit Time*, alongside Sonny Boy Williamson, with the result that his strongly jazz-tinged playing was one of B. B.'s influences. Being backed by Lockwood was proof to King that he had made it, but Lockwood extracted a high price for the honor. "His time was apeshit. I had a hard time trying to teach him," says Lockwood.[22] King confirms: "I listened to Robert Junior a lot. He taught me a lot, that way. But he used to get mad at me because he'd say, 'You'll never play nothing.' He'd beat me on the hand and say, 'Man, how come you play like that?' I'm paying him, but he'd smack me. But he's my friend and I love him. And a lot of the things he said to me made so much sense."[23]

B. B. King's first tours were sometimes very hit-and-miss affairs, and his desire to play and his resourcefulness made up for lack of experience. "Herman [Green] and I broke into his dad's church and stole his guitar," B. B. laughs. "I've never told it, publicly. We stole the guitar so we could go up to Caruthersville, Missouri, to play a job. What had happened: mine got . . . tore up. So we went in Herman's father's church. A sanctified church. Took the guitar out. So we went in there and got the guitar. Made it and played; did the job. We got to try to get it back in time to get back in the church. That was the worst thing in the world. We try to break in there without people seeing us. We not trying to take it out now; we trying to put it back in. And that's when we liked to have got caught, putting the guitar back in the church. So we did and put ten dollars in there, so his father never did know what happened. We had the guitar all night and we left ten dollars. I tease him about it every time. I didn't know it was in there. It was his idea. 'You ain't got no guitar, we'll go and get my father's guitar.' "[24]

Despite his success, B. B. King knew that he could not rely on radio alone to make a long-term career in rhythm and blues. His broadcasts as the Pepticon Boy had launched him on the local scene, but to consolidate his position it was vital to make a record. However, this new challenge was by no means an easy one to meet. In the early forties, restrictions were placed on the use of shellac, from which 78 rpm records were made but which also had military applications. The effect of this, and of a series of recording bans imposed by the all-powerful musicians' union, which feared the impact on its members' livelihoods of jukeboxes and of radio airplay of records, was to make the big companies that had dominated prewar recording unenthusiastic about a risky niche market like R&B. By 1949, shellac rationing was long gone, and a deal had been made with the union, but there were still no record companies in Memphis.

Things were very different in Chicago, New York and Los Angeles, where small companies like Aristocrat, Gotham and Aladdin had sprung up, encouraged by the appearance of the first portable tape recorders. To be a producer, all you had to do in the postwar years was buy an Ampex or Magnacord machine, and discover a star of tomorrow. When B. B. King asked Bert Ferguson about the possibility of making a record at WDIA, Ferguson looked for a reliable company, and telephoned Nashville's Jim Bulleit, whose Bullet label had done more with country music than with blues up till then.

Don Kern, the technical manager at WDIA, turned himself into a sound engineer for the occasion, and recorded King and his group on an old acetate disc cutter in the station's main studio. King was aware of the high stakes riding on this opportunity, and instead of calling on the services of his usual accompanists he decided to use an experienced bandleader, the bass player Tuff Green. Besides Green, the lineup included the brothers Thomas and Ben Branch on trumpet and saxophone respectively, a young session trombonist, Sammie Jett, and drummer Phineas Newborn Sr. The latter brought along his sons, Phineas Jr. and Calvin, to play piano and guitar; King recalls that he had to get special permission from the musicians' union to use Phineas Jr. because he was not yet eighteen years old. This was quite a lineup, for subsequently Phineas Jr. became a remarkable jazz pianist, and for a number of years Ben Branch was the bandleader for Operation Breadbasket, a movement begun by Jesse Jackson and Martin Luther King. It is Branch's melancholy claim to fame that he was the last person King spoke to before his assassination on 4 April 1968.

The use of brass, which has been a consistent feature of King's recordings, was obviously inspired by his admiration for popular artists of the day like Louis Jordan, whose brilliant and lively music he especially admired. In all, four titles were recorded ("Miss Martha King," "When Your Baby Packs Up and Goes," "Got the Blues" and "Take a Swing with Me"), and were released in the summer of 1949 on two Bullet 78s. "Miss Martha King," a tribute to his wife, was written up in July in the trade paper *Billboard*, which awarded it a mediocre fifty-three out of a hundred. As for "Got the Blues," three months later it got a disappointing forty-four, along with this comment: "Southern blues shouter may have talent, but he's obscured here by loud and loose small combo orking."[25] B. B. King obviously didn't get it together for his recording debut, as can be heard on these sides, which are of historical interest but are a long way from showing the blues genius of today. Most noticeably, although B. B.'s vocal has that characteristically frail, taut sound, his guitar stays well in the background, confined to a subsidiary, rhythmic role.

"I always said that I put that Bullet label, as it was called, out of business. It did go out of business right after that," says King jokingly.[26] From a money angle, the Bullet recordings were disappointing, for King never made a cent from his efforts in the studio. However, it was no small thing to have two records to his credit. To begin with, it was another step in his career, and gave him the status to get better terms from the clubs where he worked every weekend. Second, his radio job, and the fact that WDIA had been involved in the deal with Jim Bulleit, meant that his pair of records was guaranteed airplay, which inevitably had a beneficial effect on his popularity. Above all, though, the discs, in spite of their shortcomings, were to attract the attention of a more important record company, Modern.

Modern had been founded by Saul Bihari, who owned several bars and a jukebox business in the African-American part of Los Angeles. Immediately after the war there was a shortage of suitable records to stock his jukeboxes, and a glut of R&B bands looking for recording opportunities; these two factors prompted him to start his own company in 1946. In less than two years he was the boss of a flourishing independent company, with product ranging from jazz to country music by way of pop and, of course, rhythm and blues.

Two of Saul Bihari's brothers, Joe and Jules, were also involved in the business, and a third, Lester, was in charge of sales. In late 1949 the Biharis decided to put more effort into the R&B field, and to set up a subsidiary label; Jules went looking for talent and a name for the new label. After a public contest, broadcast by various disc jockeys, the name RPM was chosen; the new 45 rpm records had recently been introduced, and the abbreviation was in the public eye. One of the first artists signed by RPM was B. B. King, who was taking advantage of the fact that he had no contract with Bullet Records.

There are conflicting accounts of how B. B. King made contact with the Biharis. Don Kern, WDIA's technical manager, claims to have got them together by sending the Bullet records to the Biharis. Ike Turner, who was soon to be one of their main talent scouts in the Memphis area, has also been mentioned, but King expressly denies that he was involved: "I do know that when I met Ike, the first time was before either one of us ever recorded, and that was in Clarksdale, Mississippi. Then I didn't see him anymore until he was recording, and so was I. And he then was associated with the people that I started to recording with later, which was the Bihari Brothers, but Ike never did have anything to do with me."[27] Another possible go-between could have been producer Sam Phillips, who was then in close touch with the Biharis. In January 1950 Phillips had inaugurated his Memphis Recording Service at 706 Union Avenue, a few blocks from WDIA's studios, with the idea of recording local R&B artists on behalf of visiting record companies. Phillips is best known for being the first to record Elvis Presley, Jerry Lee Lewis, Carl Perkins and Johnny Cash, but in 1950 his stroke of genius was to realize that Beale Street and the Delta were bursting with talented black musicians in need of a helping hand from an enterprising company. Eventually market forces led him to concentrate on his rockabilly and rock 'n' roll roster, but before that Phillips was involved in the discovery of such major blues artists as Howlin' Wolf, Bobby Bland, Junior Parker, Earl Hooker, Rufus Thomas and Little Milton. "My work was not only to cut hit records but my purpose was to simultaneously try to get acceptance for the artistry of black people, and hopefully then we would have more people that would get interested in listening to black music," says Phillips. "The Atlantics and the Chesses and the Checkers and all of that, they were tryin' to do the same thing to a certain extent, but I knew what it took to get it. I knew where it needed to break out first, and that would be the South."[28]

However they came about, B. B. King's first recordings for RPM were made at Sam Phillips's studio. Around July 1950 he cut four titles there, and RPM put out his first release in September, on one of the newfangled 45 rpm discs. The accompaniment was much simpler than on the Bullet sides, with just a piano and rhythm section behind B. B. King's voice and guitar. This stripped-down arrangement seems to have found favor with *Billboard*, which gave "B. B. Boogie" an encouraging sixty-six.

This first release didn't achieve exceptional sales, but it did well enough to encourage the Biharis to persevere with King, who returned to 706 Union three times in the first half of 1951. Five singles were released from these sessions, and they proved that B. B. King was a musician worth watching, with each new recording confirming both his vocal and his instrumental abilities. The guitar solo on "My Baby's Gone," for instance, was a small miracle of simplicity and conciseness, cleverly spun out over a syncopated Latin rhythm, and "She's a Mean Woman" showed King to be a capable crooner. All the records sold very well in the Memphis area, where King was well known, but they failed to break out in the rest of the country.

While he was making records, B. B. King was still working in radio. His greatest moment in this area came in 1950, when one of the station's pioneer African-American disc jockeys, Maurice "Hot Rod" Hulbert left, having received a better offer from a station in Baltimore, Maryland. Since Blues Boy King was a popular attraction, Bert Ferguson asked him to take Hulbert's place, and present the *Sepia Swing Club* every afternoon between three and four o'clock. A year later,

Reverend Dwight "Gatemouth" Moore left, freeing up the daily slot between one and two, and the management asked King to replace Moore's gospel show with *Bee Bee's Jeebies*, on which he played "Dr. King, musical chaser of the blues and the heebie jeebies."

On these programs, King no longer sang on air, but simply played the hot records of the day between commercial breaks. Already a man of great honesty and integrity, the only recordings he refused to play were his own. "I played mostly blues records, because I like blues, and I am a blues player or singer rather. But I played other things. Louis Jordan was very popular, Dinah Washington, Ella Fitzgerald, Louis Armstrong. I played all of them. The only guy that got the short end of the stick on my program was me! I wouldn't play my own records, because I think it's a terrible thing if you're a disc jockey and you play your own records. Of course, I would hope that the other DJ's that was on the station would play them. I never would ask them, you know, but I was hoping that they would."[29]

All this activity at WDIA could only increase the audience for B. B. King the blues singer. He now had a pretty stable band, called the Beale Streeters because he had met most of the musicians on the sidewalks or in the clubs on Beale. Among them were Adolph "Billy" Duncan, a regular at Sam Phillips's studio; John Alexander, a piano player who later became famous as Johnny Ace, and killed himself playing Russian roulette; Earl Forrest, a fine drummer; and Bobby Bland, employed by B. B. King successively as driver, valet and relief vocalist, who was later to become one of the great names of soul music.

It was then, too, that King ran into other young musicians who were trying their luck in Memphis, like harmonica players Junior Parker and James Cotton, and even Elvis Presley. "I knew Elvis before he was popular. He used to come around and be around us a lot. There was a place we used to go and hang out at on Beale Street. People had like pawnshops there, and a lot of us used to hang out in certain of these places, and this was where I met him."[30] It's obvious from these memories that the music scene in Memphis and the Delta was very competitive.

B. B. King was now appearing live more and more, and at ever greater distances from Memphis, so that it was becoming essential for him to acquire a manager. He met Robert Henry in the latter's natural habitat, a pool hall on Beale. Henry had been working on Beale Street since 1911, and knew every café and bar owner in the Mid-South who booked bands on weekends. Thanks to Henry, King and his Beale Streeters played every week in juke joints scattered across the map: in Arkansas at Slackbritches in Birdsong, Black Willie's in Osceola, or the White Swan in Brinkley; in Covington, Tennessee, the Blue Flame; and in Jackson, Mississippi, at Stevens's Lounge. One of his favorite venues, though, was Jones' Night Spot in Indianola, where he had himself discovered so many of his peers. "Small places. They had gambling, every place had gambling, and the place would hold, maybe a hundred people, hundred and fifty at the most. They usually had one little room for gambling, and all of the swinging people would have fun dancing and playing music in the big room. They'd have food, music, boys and girls, young people and old people, it was a lot of fun."[31]

As B. B. became more and more of a traveling man, Martha King was finding it difficult to put up with his absences, as well as with the temptations her husband was subjected to by the women in his audiences; his female acquaintances sometimes made no bones about showing their affection for him, and, by 1949, one of them had even given birth to his first child. Jealousy and separation are occupational risks for show business marriages, and they were already giving B. B. and Martha problems when a crucial event threw their relationship into even deeper turmoil around Christmas 1951: "Three O'Clock Blues" on RPM 339, King's latest single, entered the *Billboard* charts on 29 December, and his career as a nationwide star was about to begin.

3
THE CHITLIN CIRCUIT
(1952-1960)

"Three O'Clock Blues" was the first of the long string of hits that has sustained B. B. King as a leading African-American musician for more than forty years. It is extraordinary that someone like King, who first appeared on the *Billboard* charts when the big names were people like Nat "King" Cole, the Clovers, Lloyd Price and Ruth Brown, should still be a contender in the hit parade during the early nineties alongside Boyz II Men, Tony! Toni! Toné!, Whitney Houston and Michael Jackson. A permanent presence of this kind in the fickle and unforgiving world of pop music is remarkable. According to *Billboard*'s figures, B. B. King appears in the Top Twenty African-American musicians at an impressive number eleven, behind James Brown, Aretha Franklin, Stevie Wonder, the Temptations, Louis Jordan, Ray Charles, Marvin Gaye, Gladys Knight, the Isley Brothers and Fats Domino. Ultimately, King owes this exceptional track record to "Three O'Clock Blues."

Unlike his previous recordings for RPM, "Three O'Clock Blues" was not made in Sam Phillips's studio. Although Phillips and Modern had worked together closely since the start of the Memphis Recording Service in January 1950, relations between the two companies went from warm to glacial when Jules Bihari realized that Phillips was offering to Leonard Chess in Chicago masters that were supposedly exclusive to Modern. After August 1951 the Biharis ceased all collaboration with Phillips, and had to come up with new ways of recording their artists in Memphis.

So it was that in the late summer, "Three O'Clock Blues" was recorded on a portable tape recorder at the Memphis YMCA on Lauderdale Street. Joe Bihari remembers this semi-improvised session well: "They had a large room with an out-of-tune upright piano. At that session, we cut Johnny Ace, Roscoe Gordon, and Bobby Bland—possibly also Ike Turner. By then we were recording on tape, not disk. Apart from B. B.'s debut hit, we got 'No More Doggin'' by Roscoe

Gordon, which came onto best-seller lists just as 'Three O'Clock' was beginning to fade."[1]

As soon as "Three O'Clock Blues," B. B. King's seventh RPM single, was released, it grabbed the attention of reviewers and disc jockeys all over the country, and their enthusiasm did a lot to make it a success. Nevertheless, to a present-day listener, it doesn't seem much different from his earlier recordings. Both the opening guitar solo and the one midway through the number are pretty unpolished, showing that B. B.'s instrumental work was still strongly influenced by Delta country blues. It was probably the extraordinary assurance of his singing and the nonchalant ease of his phrasing that gripped the record-buying public.

"Three O'Clock Blues" was not a new song; it was borrowed from the Oklahoma-born guitarist Lowell Fulson, who had briefly charted with it three years before. King was a strong admirer of Fulson, especially of his vocal work; when Fulson passed through Memphis, the two men had gotten to know one another. "B. B. King wasn't recording when I did 'Three O'Clock Blues' in '48 or '49. I gave it to him. Every time that B. B. and I get together, he always says, 'You gave me that big number,' " Fulson remembers. King, who was the only disc jockey playing Fulson's records in 1950, had come to see him when he was appearing at the racetrack in Memphis. King's plugging of Fulson over the air was so effective that a second concert had to be arranged. When King asked him for permission to record "Three O'Clock Blues," it would have been churlish of Fulson to refuse, especially since he had no idea that the young disc jockey would make it a best-seller and the foundation of his career : "He put it over beautifully. . . . His voice part was so much better than mine. It was beautiful."[2]

A few days after it was released, B. B. King's version started to sell all over the country. Two days before New Year's, it made the *Billboard* hit parade, and hauled itself into the number one spot on 2 February 1952. In all, the record spent seventeen weeks on the charts, including five at number one, placing the names of both King and RPM firmly in the minds of the public. This first success guaranteed Modern's fledgling subsidiary a long life. For B. B. King, it was the beginning of profound changes in his way of life and his conception of his music.

Unlike many artists whose first records just scrape into the charts, B. B. King had gone to number one the first time, a situation which created its own problems. In particular, the slightest false step could see him joining the ranks of the one-hit wonders. In order to last, King had to satisfy his new public in live appearances, meanwhile thinking hard about his next release. Above all, he had to stay cool while his income suddenly soared. "I had been making about $85.00 a week with my playing and being on the radio and everything else I could do—$85.00 total—and when I recorded that first big hit, I started making $2,500.00 a week."[3]

Another basic change was the need for the new R&B idol to appear in black America's larger entertainment venues. Bert Ferguson at WDIA and B. B.'s manager, Robert Henry, did their best to set this up, but running the career of such a big star was out of their league, and they decided to entrust King to one of the best-known booking agencies in the country, New York's Universal Attractions, who signed him to an exclusive contract for six months. Being exclusive, the deal would discourage the greedy attentions of other promoters; being for six months, it protected Universal in case King's career turned out to be a flash in the pan.

Under the terms of his contract, King was supported on his first national tour by Tiny Bradshaw's Orchestra, one of the most popular bands in the early fifties. Back in Memphis, B. B.'s usual backing musicians decided to carry on without him, under the leadership of John Alexander, who soon became a nationwide star under his stage name of Johnny Ace.

Historically, black America's shrines of jazz and R&B were the large theaters in the heart of the big city ghettos in the Midwest and on the East Coast. From the thirties to the late sixties, from the days of Bessie Smith and Duke Ellington to those of Gladys Knight and the O'Jays, venues like the Regal in Chicago, the Howard in Washington, the Paradise in Detroit and the Apollo in Harlem had made and unmade careers. The audiences could be generous to artists who pleased their ears, but ferocious in their disapproval of those unfortunates who didn't measure up to their standards.

As a general rule, a theater like the Apollo would put on the same show about thirty times in a week. At each of the five daily shows running from twelve noon to midnight, there would be a film, followed by a succession of musical acts introduced by comedians like Redd Foxx, who would keep the audience roaring with risqué jokes during the changeovers.

For B. B. King, appearing in this setting would be the test of his ability to capitalize on the success of "Three O'Clock Blues." He was understandably very nervous before his first show, at the Howard in Washington. Tiny Bradshaw did not help by asking him for the sheet music of his arrangements. At this time, King had absolutely no formal training in music, and on the rare occasions when he had had to work with a brass section, it had all been done by improvisation. There was no question of that with Bradshaw's eighteen-piece orchestra, though. Rescue came in the shape of Tiny Kennedy, Bradshaw's lead singer, who took a liking to King. He wrote out the sheet music, and he also made sure that B. B. bought himself a proper stage outfit: white shirt and black tuxedo. After a few days, King was sufficiently at ease on stage to win over the public, and his first tour was a complete success.

Over the following months, King continued touring the biggest theaters on the southeastern seaboard. Well aware that success can be fleeting, he hadn't quit his job at WDIA, and had asked his boss to keep a place open for him until "Three O'Clock Blues" had started to fade, and he could go back to broadcasting. Bert Ferguson was only too glad to agree, for he knew how his station could benefit from having such a famous presenter. But nothing could stop King's rise to fame, it seemed. After recording two new singles for RPM in January 1952, he came back to the mikes at the end of the winter to make "You Didn't Want Me" and "You Know I Love You." This session took place at Tuff Green's house, with his band supplying the accompaniment. On 13 September, "You Know I Love You" entered the charts, and reached number one in November. Unlike "Three O'Clock Blues," this latest hit was a sugary ballad spotlighting B. B. King's talents as a crooner, and was a long way from his Mississippi roots. Yet again, his guitar was notable for its reticence, proving once more that his audience saw King primarily as a vocalist.

The importance of Jules Bihari in building B. B. King's career has been insufficiently appreciated. It was Jules, rather than King, who usually decided on the arrangements and the musicians, and sometimes it was his ideas that decided the repertoire, as his brother Joe explained in a rare interview: "On some songs, they had them in their head, but couldn't quite get it together, and there was help. We worked with artists in recording sessions. . . . You might notice the name of Jules Taub on some songs. That was a pseudonym for Jules Bihari, who worked with the artists."[4]

In the early days, Bihari/Taub favored the more refined, sentimental ballads over the Mississippi blues. This was a logical stance in the early fifties, when the honeyed delivery of Nat "King" Cole, the slick arrangements of Joe Liggins, and the Clovers' vocal harmonies dominated the market. This made all the more sense in that hitherto Modern had emphasized singers like Jimmy Witherspoon and Helen Humes. However, it was a time when record buyers' tastes were changing fast, and soon the upper reaches of the hit parade were occupied by new artists, with tougher styles and rougher voices, and names like Big Mama Thornton, Little Walter and Eddie Boyd.

In February 1952, journalist Hal Webman described for *Billboard* readers the changes that were taking place: "For the first time in many months, the down-home, Southern-style blues appears to have taken a solid hold in the current rhythm and blues record market. Down-home blues had been taking a back seat in the market to the big city blues, good rocking novelties and vocal quartet ballads for quite a while. However, the Southern market appears to have opened up to its widest extent in some time, and the lowdown stuff has been cropping up as best-selling wax of late. Such artists as B. B. King, Howlin' Wolf, Roscoe Gordon, Fats Domino, Sonny Boy Williamson, Lightnin' Hopkins, John Lee Hooker, Lloyd [sic] Fulson, Billy Wright, Muddy Waters, etc., have taken a fast hold in such market areas as New Orleans, Dallas, Atlanta, Los Angeles, etc. Even the sophisticated big towns like New York and Chicago have felt the Southern blues influence in wax tastes."[5]

Under the guidance of Jules Bihari, who always paid close attention to market trends, B. B. King's repertoire moved gradually towards the formula that was to make his fortune and him an original artist. From mid-1953, King laid aside the ballads to become one of the true creators of modern blues. "Blind Love," recorded in Houston in June 1953 is a good example of B. B. King's eventual style, combining the Delta blues with sophisticated, elegant guitar and vocal phrasing. The lyrics still dealt with the characteristic rural blues theme of a woman both idealized and unfaithful, but, in terms of rhythm, "Blind Love" was a medium-fast shuffle typical of the R&B bands of the day; built around a piano, bass and drums rhythm section, it featured a four-piece brass section that punctuated each verse.

But the great innovation was the appearance of B. B. King's guitar in the forefront of the music, a change announced by the intro, a biting single-note guitar solo. Another guitar chorus followed the second verse, seeming to be a dramatic expression of the story that was unfolding. No longer an accompanying instrument, B. B. King's guitar was becoming an extension of his voice, while the short, lyrical phrases with which it rounded off each sung line were reminiscent of the Pentecostal churches, and the way a congregation in the throes of spirit possession would respond to the preacher's every utterance. With "Blind Love," B. B. King signalled that he was no longer content to be simply a gifted vocalist like his old associates Bobby Bland and Johnny Ace; he was now asserting his status as a hugely talented artist, who used his guitar as much as his voice to express the essence of the blues.

If one examines B. B. King's recorded output between 1951 and 1956, the transformation is glaringly obvious. Out of sixty songs, sixteen appeared in the *Billboard* charts for varying periods of time, beginning with the ballads "You Know I Love You" and "Story from My Heart and Soul." Apart from "Sneakin' Around," a modest hit in 1955, which showcased King the crooner, the other sides were firmly in the traditional blues field, alternating slow numbers ("When My Heart

Beats Like a Hammer," "Ten Long Years," "Sweet Little Angel") with shuffles along the lines of "Blind Love" ("Please Love Me," "Please Hurry Home," "You Upset Me Baby," "Whole Lotta Love," "Every Day I Have the Blues," "Crying Won't Help You," "Bad Luck"). Also among the hits, it should be noted, was "Woke Up This Morning," a remake of "My Baby's Gone," which had been among King's first RPM recordings, here given a Latin feel by the use of jazzy Afro-Cuban rhythms.

What made B. B. King so original, aside from the important role given to his guitar, was the way in which he modernized the Delta blues, even though he stayed faithful to its musical structure. The main agent of the transformation was the songs' arrangements, which forged a strong link between the rough-and-ready traditional sounds of Mississippi and the big band jazz that had played an important part in the development of rhythm and blues from the forties onwards. The words of King's songs had also been brought up to date. For the most part, his repertoire was borrowed, rather than original; thus John Lee "Sonny Boy" Williamson's "Million Years Blues" became "When My Heart Beats Like a Hammer," and the traditional country blues theme popularized by Tommy McClennan, "Bottle It Up and Go," became "Shake It Up and Go." In his versions of numbers like these, B. B. King usually took out any references to violence and sexuality; these were common themes in prewar blues, but he wanted to avoid giving offence to an upwardly mobile audience, which was already turning its back on traditional blues, perceiving it as violent, countrified and old-fashioned.

There are many instances of such changes: in "Baby Look at You," King changes Wynonie Harris's line "You wanna pull your knife and cut me" to "You wanna jump on me and hurt me"; in "I Gotta Find My Baby," originally a Doctor Clayton song, he omits a verse which mentions cocaine and reefers, not wishing to shock listeners who were striving to escape their harsh ghetto environment and had no great wish to be reminded of their roots. King was also anxious not to arouse the hostility of those well-meaning groups in the African-American community who already looked unfavorably on the blues. They didn't care for his single "You Upset Me Baby," for instance; this slightly ribald description of an ideal woman was banned from airplay after it was criticized in the trade paper *Variety*. "Still sold over a million of 'em," chuckled King at the time.[6]

It's undeniable that B. B. King's success was the climax of his development as an interpreter, rather than the triumph of an originator. "Three O'Clock Blues," a hit for Lowell Fulson three years before King's version, was the first instance. During his career with Modern, King was to repeat the process several times. Early in

1955, "Every Day I Have the Blues" was an example of this. Composed by the Sparks Brothers, Aaron and Milton, who recorded it for Bluebird in 1935, "Every Day" was a big hit for Memphis Slim in 1948 as "Nobody Loves Me." Two years later, Lowell Fulson gave the song a definitive reading, and restored its original title, before King made it one of his warhorses. Although he mainly drew on Fulson's version for inspiration, King was equally well aware of vocalist Joe Williams's reading of the song, recorded with King Kolax's Orchestra. Later, Williams would remake a hit version of it with Count Basie.

A further good example of the way in which blues themes both persist and evolve is "Sweet Little Angel," which was a sizeable hit for B. B. King in late 1956, twenty-six years after the release of Lucille Bogan's original version, "Black Angel Blues," on Brunswick. In 1934 Tampa Red, one of the most heavily recorded artists of the twenties and thirties, recorded a very influential version of this blues. His clean, elegant style made its mark on Robert Nighthawk, a Delta blues innovator whom Riley King had met around Indianola; in his turn, Nighthawk brought the theme up to date when he recorded it for the Chess brothers while visiting Chicago in 1949. In 1953, Nighthawk's most gifted pupil, Earl Hooker, recorded a remarkable version of "Sweet Black Angel"; three years later, B. B. King put the finishing touches to Lucille Bogan's song.

In his elaborately arranged version, King was careful to avoid any racial connotation. In those early days of Reverend Martin Luther King's struggle for civil rights, any reference to blackness could be seen as a retrograde step by a community looking for its identity. "I got the idea for 'Sweet Little Angel' from Robert Nighthawk's 'Sweet Black Angel,' though I later discovered that the song had been recorded by someone before Nighthawk. At the time 'black' was not a popular word, as it is now. Instead of using the old title, I changed it to 'Sweet Little Angel'—and that was a pretty big record for me."[7]

His string of hits, from "Three O'Clock Blues" to "Sweet Little Angel," made B. B. King one of the most in-demand artists on the African-American music scene in the fifties. During the first two years of his stardom, King would head back to Memphis between tours, to his wife and his WDIA broadcasts. "Like weekends I would go. I would go like to Atlanta. In fact, I've even went to Washington. I would go to the West Coast. Went to Los Angeles once during that time. But I'd leave like on Friday night and get off for that next day. Then play on Saturday night and then I worked back. So I didn't go far. But I was always going some place like St. Louis. I'd go there very easy. St. Louis, Atlanta, Houston. But most of the time it was within a hundred, two hundred mile radius."[8]

The ceaseless touring created tensions, and ultimately conflict, both at work and in his marriage. A crisis point was reached in the family circle first: Martha asked for a divorce in 1952, bringing an eight-year marriage to an end. The fact that they had no children probably had as much to do with it as King's frantic work rate. Martha was jealous of her husband's wandering life, and reacted badly to the adoration he received from female fans. All musicians recognize the difficulties that life on the road poses for married couples, and Riley and Martha were no exception to the rule. King was deeply affected for a long time by the fact that his job had destroyed his marriage. Despite many opportunities to meet women in his travels, he was for a good while reluctant to think about remarrying.

His divorce from WDIA came at the end of 1953, but in a calmer atmosphere. The break was due more to outside factors than to a deliberate decision by WDIA's management. Because of his popularity with listeners to the Memphis station, King had signed an advertising contract early in his radio career with the makers of Lucky Strike cigarettes. WDIA's management had been very glad of this contract, for national brands had reacted coolly until then, and Lucky Strike was the first sponsor to take the risk. "When we tried to go through the New York agencies, we had a lot of resistance," John Pepper, one of the founders of WDIA, recalls. "I remember [when] they bought B. B. King fifteen minutes a day across the board, that was their first adventure into this kind of advertising . . . the first time they put their foot in the water."[9]

If the figures are to be believed, this experiment paid off, for the Lucky Strike contract opened the door to a number of other agreements with national advertisers. WDIA's papers show, in fact, that the company had more of them signed up in the fifties than any other independent radio station. Nevertheless, B. B. King was about to be a victim of his own success. His tours meant that he could no longer make live broadcasts regularly, and when he was doing concerts a long way from Memphis, the program director had got into the habit of broadcasting recorded shows in an attempt to fool listeners into thinking that the Blues Boy was on air live. "We had the intro, his commercials and his other things and we'd just work it all together and it was supposed to be live. We even sent air checks off," recalls David James Mattis, then the program director.[10] This system worked perfectly until Lucky Strike sent someone to check that the show it sponsored was running smoothly, and found out about the deception. WDIA lost Lucky Strike's advertising, and they and King came to a mutual agreement to end their relationship. King's old friend Rufus Thomas had the difficult job of taking over the broadcasts, and soon became one of the station's most popular personalities.

For B. B. King, the end of his association with WDIA was annoying, but it seemed inevitable, given the way his career was taking off. WDIA represented five vital years of his life, and the faithful support of people like Bert Ferguson, who had trusted him enough to hire him in late 1948. "Mr. Ferguson was a gem," says King. "He was one of the nicest people that I've ever known in my life. Mr. Ferguson said to all of the personnel—'You are Mr., if you are Mr. You are Mrs., if you are Mrs. But other than that you are people and employees of the station,'—and that's the first time I ever heard that before in my life in the South."[11]

The end of his career as a disc jockey was more of a blow to King's morale than to his pocket, however. Since his first tour for Universal Attractions, there hadn't been enough hours in the day to deal with the demands of his fans. Since he didn't have his own band, King's main problem was to find a competent and reliable group of musicians for his live shows. Shortly after leaving WDIA, he made a deal with Bill Harvey, a saxophonist who was leading the house band at the Club Handy, and who was called by King in his autobiography "the George Washington of Memphis musicians."

Harvey was a first-class musician and an experienced arranger, and the two men decided to join forces. Henceforth, King appeared with six musicians, directed by Harvey. "I didn't have a group," King says. "From '52, I believe, to '55 I was featured like that you know. . . . [Bill] Harvey and I thought we had a pretty good combination so we then decided that we would go to Buffalo Booking Agency along with the lady that owned it called Evelyn Johnson. . . . Evelyn Johnson agreed to book us for X amount and this is how Bill and I came together. But still it wasn't my band."[12]

The Buffalo Booking Agency, which was based in Houston, was no ordinary company. Unlike its competitors, it was run by a woman and owned by a black businessman, Don Robey. Robey had begun his career as the owner of the Bronze Peacock, a large club in the African-American part of Houston. He had then become interested in the record business, and founded the Peacock label in the late forties. A few years later, Robey bought the Duke label from David James Mattis, WDIA's program director; over the next ten years he built up one of the most important independent companies in the fields of rhythm and blues and gospel music, drawing heavily on Memphis talent. Before Berry Gordy and Motown, along with Jimmy Bracken and Vivian Carter in Chicago and Leon and Otis René in Los Angeles, Don Robey was one of the first African-American businessmen to get involved in the record industry. Among the artists he recorded were Clarence "Gatemouth" Brown, Johnny Otis, Big Mama Thornton, Johnny Ace, Bobby Bland and Junior Parker.

As a counterpart to his recording activities, Robey soon decided to set up a booking agency to mount tours for his main stars, and also for other big names in the R&B field who were looking, like B. B. King, for a set-up that would do a good job of looking after their interests. To this end, he founded the Buffalo agency, and put his long-serving aide, Evelyn Johnson, in charge.

Mrs. Johnson was a decisive and able businesswoman who had the interests of her artists at heart. With her to push, B. B. King's career became even bigger business, as offers of engagements flowed in from all over the country. With his RPM recordings entering the hit parade, he became a mainstay of the chitlin circuit, the network of African-American theaters and clubs nicknamed after a soul food dish made from hogs' intestines.

The circuit had first sprung up along the north-south line of communication between New Orleans and Chicago, which is marked by the Mississippi River, Highways 51 and 61, and the tracks of the Illinois Central Railroad. From this spine, the chitlin circuit branched off all across the Old South and to the cities of the Atlantic coast. This structure enabled blues artists to work in Louisiana and Florida during the winter, thus escaping the rigors of winter in the Northeast and the Midwest. Since the late forties, the network had also spread westward to the Pacific coast, across Texas, New Mexico and Arizona.

There were several levels to the chitlin circuit. The small clubs and country juke joints where lesser-known musicians worked from day to day had none of the sophistication found in the posh Chicago lounges, the Royal Peacock in Atlanta, or the Howard Theater in Washington. For the overwhelming majority of blues artists, the chitlin circuit meant violence and danger, as Big Moose Walker, a regular in these cutthroat dives, recalls: "We played in Lambert, Mississippi, we played Cleveland, we played Leland, we played in Brooksville, all in Mississippi. We played juke houses, all out in different places, barns and stuff cut in two, just anywhere. And I seen guys get killed for fifteen cents. They would kill you for a dime, you know, for a dime!"[13]

B. B. King knew this side of the chitlin circuit well; he had done most of his playing there in the early years of his career. After "Three O'Clock Blues," he had gone up a step, appearing almost exclusively in the best small-town clubs and the most important theaters in the cities. "We played the big theaters like the Palace Theater in Memphis or the Howard in Washington, but we also played the smaller clubs in the little towns. Like Indianola, where I grew up, they had a place there called Jones' Night Spot, that was later called Club Ebony. If you played Arkansas, you had Slackbritches, you had Hick's Corner. In Greenville, Mississippi, you had the Elks, each one of these places was a little nightclub. In Mobile, Alabama, you had Club Harlem, Sunbeam Mitchell's in Memphis or the Dew Drop in New Orleans. In Chicago we would play the Burning Spear, and you would never stay more than a couple nights in each one of these clubs, so you just traveled from one to the other."[14]

The comfort of the surroundings wasn't the only difference between the squalid juke joints of the Deep South and the well-to-do big-city clubs. In the former, musicians usually played for the gate, although a two-hundred-to-three-hundred-dollar minimum was usually guaranteed in the places where B. B. King and Bill Harvey worked. That didn't stop some promoters from running off with the takings at the end of the evening and neglecting to pay the musicians. All the veterans of the chitlin circuit say that the public was sometimes hard to please, but getting paid could be even harder.

The guitarist Clarence "Gatemouth" Brown remembers a concert like that—as it happens, one where he was sharing the bill with B. B. King: "I remember one time we had about 3,500 people in the house and this guy didn't want to pay off nobody. Had a big .45 sittin' on the table and he didn't know I had a pistol in my pocket. So I pulled my pistol and I laid it right up above his head. I told B. B. to count his money out and count mine, too. And he did and I backed out the door with my gun, just like the wild west days. I hollered at my driver, I said, 'Get this Pontiac rollin'!' He had the motor runnin', I got in that car and we burned rubber from there back to Texas."[15]

Things didn't always reach that level, but some promoters would use any excuse to get out of paying the artists. "They'd tell you their wife had died. Their children had pneumonia. I once had a dude come say to me he couldn't make it 'cause he had four flat tires!" King says.[16] "A lot of the promoters couldn't afford to pay you very much money, and if they didn't have a pretty good crowd, sometimes you didn't get paid at all," B. B. adds. "I only have about $180,000 owed up to me from my playing during my career. I'd say 90% of the promoters were for real, just like they are today. But then you had the other 10%—the young promoter, probably his first time to give a dance or concert. If he didn't make it, that was it, because he had thrown in everything he had to do this one concert which he felt would be a gold mine. He'd say to himself, 'Well, if I can get B. B. King or Junior Parker or whoever, *this* night they're going to pull me through,' and a lot of times that didn't happen, and when it didn't happen for that promoter, you didn't find him. He wasn't around afterwards."[17]

Success meant doing more and more concerts, some in parts of the country where King hadn't performed before. In March 1952, for instance, the promoter Ben Waller set up a concert in Los Angeles, at which King shared the bill both with young artists like Pee Wee Crayton and the brilliant singer-composer Percy Mayfield and with idols of his like Roy Milton and Joe Liggins. In February 1954 he returned to California for his first proper tour on the West Coast, and made a triumphal appearance in Los Angeles, to match those he had made in the New Mexico and Arizona towns he had passed through en route. In Los Angeles, the crowd trying to get into the 5–4 Ballroom was so dense that the police, fearing trouble, broadcast radio appeals on a black-oriented station for people to stay at home. When King returned to Hollywood the following August to appear at the Savoy Ballroom, the promoters had again underestimated public interest, and more than three thousand people were turned away from the doors. Faced with such phenomenal events, the trade press noted admiringly that King's talent was so exceptional that his popularity had grown continuously since his first nationwide hit; *Billboard* cited as proof the record audience of ten thousand who had crammed into Houston's city auditorium to hear him in May 1954.

King's financial position improved along with his career, of course, and from 1954 he was one of the top ten earners in the R&B field. Always a sharp dresser, he now had an impressive wardrobe which included a large number of tuxedos and suits, as well as less conservative garments. A picture taken in the mid-fifties by noted Memphis photographer Ernest Withers shows King on stage with a flashy jacket, two-tone shoes and a showy pair of Bermuda shorts!

On 27 November 1954, King celebrated five busy years of recording in the company of the chief executives of Modern Records, Evelyn Johnson, and the staff of the Buffalo Booking Agency, who wanted to pay tribute to one of their most go-getting artists. In its report of this event, *Billboard* noted that "King has established an enviable record in both the disk market and on the personal appearance circuit. Evelyn Johnson of the Buffalo Booking Agency estimates that King has played to an average attendance of 325,000 people, grossing approximately $480,000."[18]

The downside of this dizzy rise to fame was fatigue, which built up with the number of concerts he played and the long journeys from one club to the next. In this respect, 1956 outdid all other years. The first day of January found B. B. starting a thirty-date tour in Florida, and he kept up this alarming pace the whole year: in all, he made 342 appearances in 366 days, an all-time record for which he was presented with a gold ring by his booking agency. Considering that King also had to make new records, and accordingly had three separate studio sessions in Los Angeles during the year, it is not hard to understand that such a work rate must have been almost unbearable.

This was all the more so in that since the end of 1955 King had had an additional responsibility. After working closely with him for three years, Bill Harvey had been forced by ill health to give up his job as bandleader. Even though his natural shyness made him feel that he wasn't cut out for leading a band, the situation left King no alternative but finally to put together a team of his own, and purchase a touring vehicle. To a music fan like him who had stood with an open mouth when his idols Count Basie or Lucky Millinder drove through Indianola in their customized buses, owning a big Aero was synonymous with prestige and success. As for his new group, it included a number of alumni of Bill Harvey's band, like the saxophonist Evelyn Young, and Earl Forrest, who had been King's very first drummer, as well as newcomers like alto saxist Johnny Board and bass player James "Shinny" Walker.

Apart from musicians, King's organization included a road manager and his assistant, a driver for the recently acquired tour bus, Big Red, and a chauffeur for King, who went from place to place separately in his Cadillac. As well as being an ambassador for the blues, he was now also running a business. "King is a wealthy man today," asserted a contemporary account of the king of the blues, going on to say that B. B. "has his personal valet to care for nearly 100 suits of clothes, owns two Cadillacs and recently presented Caddys to each member of his seven-piece band as a Christmas gift, and has installed his parents, three sisters and one brother on that 'patch of land' 25 miles from Memphis."[19] A truly generous person, King indeed insisted on purchasing a 150-acre farm for his father just outside of Memphis. Over the years, Riley and Albert Lee King would enjoy a continuous and tight relationship, even though the father was just as private as his son. But in time of need, B. B. could always turn to his elder for advice, or even just for a sympathetic ear.

In the mid-fifties, B. B.'s minimum per concert went from five hundred to seven hundred dollars, and soon broke the symbolic one-thousand-dollar barrier. This not only boosted the size of B. B.'s income, it also let him increase the size of his band, which by then numbered around a dozen musicians, thanks to the brass section which was to support him in the future. King's first opportunity to work with a large outfit had been with the house band at the Palace Theatre in Memphis early in his career, but his fondness for the big band sound went back even further, as he explains: "I guess one of the reasons is my being brought up in the church. I can always hear the choir singing behind me, and that's what I hear when the horns are playing behind me."[20]

Among the high points at this time of good fortune was a tour of the southern states with Louis Jordan, one of the idols of his youth. In Memphis, recognition came from the African-American Chamber of Commerce, which asked him to become an honorary member. Also in Memphis, an admirer and former pupil came to pay tribute to him: Elvis Presley, who was in the process of becoming the most famous musician in the country, was eager to express publicly his sincere admiration for the guitarist during a charity concert organized by WDIA in 1956.

In an account published by the local daily newspaper, a journalist reported: "Those who were in earshot said that Presley was heard telling King, 'Thanks man for the early lessons you gave me.'"[21] Also present was photographer Ernest Withers, who recorded their meeting in a photograph which has since become world famous. "I'll tell you something else," B. B. laughs. "The first time that I ever had a picture taken with Elvis Presley, I had on the same jacket I'm wearing on my first album, the very first album titled *Singing the Blues*. No kidding. That's the best one I had!"[22]

As if 1956 had not been busy enough, it was notable for another important event, the inauguration of Blues Boy's Recording Company, owned by King, and with an appropriate address at 164 Beale Street. In its issue of 15 December 1956, *Billboard* reported: "B. B. King has formed a record label of his own, to be called Blues Boy Kingdom [sic]. Since he is still under contract to RPM himself, the talent that will be recorded will be confined to new talent that King discovers in the course of his extensive tours all over the country."[23]

To understand this development, it must be remembered that B. B. King has always been a long-term and committed blues fan. Anyone who has seen him traveling with a briefcase full of tapes by people like Blind Lemon Jefferson, Doctor Clayton, and Lloyd Glenn will realize that, international star though he is, he is still an evangelist for the music. Since childhood his admiration for the musicians whose blues lore he soaked up has been unqualified, even as he has become the most creative postwar blues artist. He had already put his talents at the disposal of others several times by 1956, most notably his old master, Sonny Boy Williamson, whom he accompanied on some November 1954 recordings made in Jackson, Mississippi, for Trumpet Records.

King didn't confine his help to established musicians. Several people who started out in the fifties remain deeply grateful to him for the advice and expertise, as well as the moral, and sometimes financial, support he has always been ready to lavish on them. The late Larry Davis recounted how B. B. unselfishly supported his emulators: "B. B. was the only person that I followed in the fifties. We came back from California in '56. B. B. was still playing Little Rock and El Dorado, Pine Bluff, which is smaller towns in Arkansas. We would follow B. B. down to Camden, which is about a hundred and ten miles from Little Rock, and from there to El Dorado, which is about thirty-five miles. And that would be as far as we would go, because we didn't have any money. B. B. wasn't making a great deal of money, but he would always give us money for gas, expenses, you know, because we would just be there with him."[24]

To King's way of thinking, it was natural to do everything possible to perpetuate the blues, and setting up a record company devoted to the music seemed a useful way to go about doing so. "You see, I felt the blues just wasn't getting a break and there were artists who probably would never get any exposure, so I started up the record label mainly to help others get a break. I wanted to keep the sound to a bluesy feel, but my main interest was to help local talent, so I set out looking for artists,"[25] he explains.

The first artist signed to Blues Boys Kingdom was a singer and harmonica player from Uniontown, Alabama, named James Levi Sebury. "I first heard Levi down in Alabama and I thought he had great blues potential. I intended to do quite a few sides with him. I thought he could be my answer to Sonny Boy Williamson."[26] Fate took a hand, though, for on 12 January 1957, just a few days after the release of "Motherless Child" and "Boogie Beat" by Levi Seabury [sic] on BBK 101, the singer, not yet thirty years old, was killed in a car crash.

Over the succeeding months, three more records appeared on Blues Boys Kingdom, respectively by Milliard Lee, who was then the regular pianist in King's band, vocal group the Five Stars, and singer Rosetta Perry, formerly with Lionel Hampton's Orchestra. B. B. had met her through his sax player, Johnny Board, and she opened the show for him when he was touring. "Rosetta was a tall shapely girl who sounded as great as she looked. I believe she was going out with Jimmy Merrit of Hamp's band. That was when Johnny Board was on sax for him, too."[27]

King also recalled recording a couple of gospel outfits; a release by a Memphis male quartet, the Bells of Harmony, did appear on Kingdom—a shortened version of the original label—but the company finally ceased operations in late 1957 or early 1958, more because of internal politics than any lack of success. "I started it. I had another great guy as the director. Honeymoon Garner and another guy called James Wilson . . . But by me being out trying to make money to keep the company going, the people that I had was so critical of people that came in, until the very ones that would have been used was the ones that were turned away. They always wanted the professional singer. They meant well but they couldn't evidently see Levi Sebury was one of the few. I guess had it not been that I heard him and liked him myself that we probably wouldn't have had him."[28]

Obviously, B. B. King was not immune from problems and worries; the end of Blues Boys Kingdom is one proof of that. His troubles were often a result of the frantic pace of his life. The chief negative aspect of success was the permanent tiredness and stress that weighed on King and his musicians. The band's day usually started with a ten- or fifteen-hour ride in the bus, after which they had to set up on stage; this would be followed by a three-to-five hour concert, and then they would dismantle and repack everything before setting off for the next town. The long distances between engagements often meant that the musicians had no chance to sleep in a bed for several days at a time.

Another source of problems was segregation, still very much in force in the South of the mid-fifties. More than once, King and his companions had to put up with hotels and restaurants that turned them away or would only serve them sandwiches in the kitchen, as well as with racist police officers who harassed and humiliated them almost daily. The bus driver soon figured out a way around the problem, however; when he stopped at a service station for gas, he would always ask for a full tank and food for everyone, knowing that the attendant's greed would usually be stronger than his racism.

King noted, though, that he didn't have difficulties from this quarter while performing: "We don't play for white people and that may be the reason why we don't run into any trouble. Of course a few whites come to hear us on one-night stands but they are so few that we never run into the segregation problem that got [Nat] King Cole in trouble in Birmingham [Alabama]."[29]

Violence was also a near daily worry on the road. Over the years, the band's history was punctuated with skirmishes. Sometimes, mobs of white men with an annoying tendency to see black musicians as fair game were the cause of pitched battles. On other occasions, jealous husbands would give violent expression to their disapproval of their wives hanging around the band members. King remembers an epic concert in Texas, which ended with a fistfight between the musicians and some audience members, armed and angry.

Finally, the road is a dangerous place in its own right, and seldom leaves those who choose to live on it unscathed. In the course of his career, B. B. King has survived fifteen car and bus wrecks, the most serious of which left him with an open wound on his right arm and a number of severed ligaments. After undergoing a major operation, King insisted on fulfilling his engagement the same evening, hammering on the strings with his left hand, since his right was temporarily useless.

The most spectacular accident was certainly the collision with a tanker which finished off Big Red, the band's tour bus, in 1958. The two people in the tanker were killed when it exploded, but B. B. King's musicians were lucky enough to escape with minor injuries. Big Red was a total loss, however. To compound the bad luck, King's insurance company had just gone bust; he had to buy a new bus and pay out a huge amount to cover his liability.

One of B. B. King's chief virtues has always been his determination to carry out his obligations and responsibilities. There are not many people in the business as conscientious as he is, or who can lay claim to missing so few concerts. In a forty-five-year career, King is proud that he has cancelled fewer than twenty engagements. This record is probably unbeatable, given that he has performed an average of 330 times a year since starting out. To his musicians, he is a trustworthy employer who pays his men well, and is always ready to help and advise those who are loyal to him; it takes a very serious blunder—the use of hard drugs is one—for him to fire a band member. And, unlike many bandleaders, King never sees it as desertion or treachery if an accompanist leaves, and even encourages them to strike out on their own if they have the motivation, ambition and ability to do so.

His loyal character is seen in the way he stayed with Modern Records through the fifties. It was King's consciousness of his debt to the Biharis that led him to keep renewing his three-year contracts until 1962. He didn't negotiate with experienced businessmen like the Bihari brothers with his eyes closed, however; friendship is one thing, business another. On two occasions he put pressure on Modern a few months before his contract was due to expire, by recording a few sides for another label.

In 1953, Don Robey, the boss of Peacock Records, was a natural choice for this tactic. King was already working for him via the Buffalo Booking Agency; in addition, the Biharis no longer had a studio readily available in Memphis, and had taken to recording him at Bill Holford's ACA studio in Houston, which Robey used for his own artists. Robey was obviously well aware of King's potential at this critical point in his career, and would have been more than happy to add him to his roster of stars. B. B. King knew how to take advantage of the rivalry between the two companies. "I wanted $5,000 from the Bihari brothers . . . and somebody didn't want me to have it," he reported later to Living Blues. "I didn't think that was such a big amount of money for that time, because I had been a very consistent seller of records. Never the big, two or three million copies like some artists.

But I'd been a consistent seller. . . . At this particular time I wanted to buy a new house, and I wanted a new bus, and several things. I could use this money for it, I thought. So then I asked if I could have it, they said, 'Oh no, not at this time.' Well, I knew that Peacock and Chess wanted me all the time. They would tell me if ever you, you know, are not with the company you're with, we'd like to have you. So I remember going to the president of Peacock, Don Robey, and I said: 'Well, my contract has just run out, and I want $5,000, and I can't get it, so if you give me $5,000, you got B. B. King.' He said, 'When do you wanna record?' So I said, 'Soon as you want.' And, I guess knowing that I'm quite loyal to whomever I'm with, they wanted to get me started as soon as possible. So he gave me $5,000. When they gave me $5,000 I say, 'OK, I've got some songs we can start recording.'

"Well, at that time, the Bihari brothers found out. They say, 'Oh, we know . . . we just need a little time.' I said, 'Well, too late now.' They said: 'Well if we buy it back, give them their money back, and give you $7,000, would you change your mind.' I said, 'Tomorrow.' So what they did was give Peacock the $5,000 back, bought and paid for the session, and gave me $7,000. And I didn't go with Peacock."[30]

According to everyone who had dealings with them, Saul Bihari and his brothers were shrewd businessmen, not keen to squander company money, and not only where payment to their artists was concerned. Kay Holford, who owned the ACA studio with her husband, Bill, still smiles at the memory. "They always paid their bills with us, but they were too cheap to pay for a hotel room to sleep in. They slept on the couches in our studio."[31]

After their run-in with Don Robey, the Biharis decided to keep King out of temptation's way by no longer using the Holfords' studio. This decision coincided with the opening by Modern of new premises in Culver City, California, in May 1954, where King would henceforth make all his recordings for the company.

However, that wasn't enough to stop a repeat of the Peacock episode in 1958, this time with the Chess brothers. Leonard and Phil Chess, who owned one of the most important black music labels, cut a few sides by King and his band a few months before his contract was due for renewal. Just as had happened five years before, an amicable settlement was reached, and the Biharis bought the masters from Chess. "Recession Blues," a superb piece of social comment which contrasted sharply with King's more romantic numbers, was released a few months later on Kent, the subsidiary label which had replaced RPM in 1958.

In the early sixties, B. B. King was still recording like clockwork for the Biharis, and putting a handful of titles into the hit parade every year. 1959 was to be a notable exception, however, as a year when, for the first time since "Three O'Clock Blues," there was no sign at all of his name in the *Billboard* charts. It's evident from listening to King's output at this time that the last few months of the decade were dominated by ballads, rather than the carefully crafted blues that had been his trademark.

With Jules Bihari in charge, the singer-guitarist was prone to forget what he was best at, and to wander, not very successfully, into easy listening territory. Trying in vain to imitate Frank Sinatra or Dean Martin, Brook Benton or Nat Cole, B. B. King lost touch with his artistic integrity on a series of mushy, sentimental numbers like "I Love You So," "Time to Say Goodbye," "The Fool" and "The Silent Prayer," which were notable mainly for their fussy arrangements and their throwaway lyrics. It's obvious that this policy was unsuccessful, for the public wanted nothing whatever to do with these insipid songs, apart from "Please Accept My Love," which reached number nine on the *Billboard* R&B charts at the end of 1958.

Jules Bihari could hardly fail to realize that he was taking an unwise artistic direction, and he made a rapid return to the blues. The first record to restore his flagship artist to success in 1960 was "Sweet Sixteen," a magnificent adaptation of a number by vocalist Big Joe Turner, and one of King's greatest hits. The song wasn't exactly a novelty, as is proved by a reference to the Korean War in the lyrics, and King had already made a number of variants of it, the most recent of them called "Sweet Thing." However, if the words of "Sweet Sixteen" were close to those of this prototype version, their arrangements had nothing in common; the busy brass of "Sweet Thing" gave way to a perfect balance between B. B.'s voice and guitar, Milliard Lee's piano trills, and the rhythm section playing a very simple 4/4 beat.

Judging by the welcome the song received, its African-American audience saw itself portrayed there. Entering the *Billboard* black charts on 18 January 1960, "Sweet Sixteen" stayed there for fourteen weeks, climbing rapidly to the number two spot, and becoming one of King's masterworks. To this day it plays a prominent part in his live performances. "I know that some people think of 'Sweet Little Angel' as my identifying song," King says. "It does play a big part. But to me, not as big as 'Sweet Sixteen' and 'Three O'Clock Blues.' 'Sixteen' was Joe Turner's tune. I recorded it in '58. But I had been hearing it before then. I found that certain artists like Louis Jordan, Joe Turner, Charles Brown—when they finished with a song, it's not wise to come up behind them until people have practically forgotten their treatment. And so when I liked a song, I'd hide it and keep it until I felt that the momentum had died on theirs."[32]

Rarely have the blues that arise from a difficult relationship between a man and a woman been better expressed. "When I first met you, baby, baby, you was just sweet sixteen / You just left your home then, woman, the sweetest thing I ever seen," begins a rapturous King, who then reveals his adored one's true face: "But you wouldn't do nothing, baby, you wouldn't do anything I asked you to / You know you ran away from your home, baby, and now you wanna run away from old B too." Nostalgia for the first moments of love, a woman's failure to understand, a man's surrender, wounded male pride that feels it must protest, family break-up and loneliness: in a few simple words, "Sweet Sixteen" draws a picture of the sociology of black America, accurately and without complacency.

In the same vein was another important song of King's from this period, a self-critical blues called "It's My Own Fault," based on a John Lee Hooker number. It was to become one of his songs most often performed by other artists, especially in Chicago, where it fitted perfectly into the city's electric blues sound.

Hard on the heels of "Sweet Sixteen," three more recordings were best-sellers in 1960, "Walkin' Dr. Bill," "Partin' Time" and "Got a Right to Love My Baby." The latter title, a slow shuffle, was in marked contrast to "Sweet Sixteen," with brassy orchestration taking over as the driving force from the guitar/piano/bass/drums set-up. In this respect, "Got a Right" was a perfect example of the way B. B. King's music had been moving for some time. Even in live performance, the modest lineup led by Bill Harvey had given way to King's own thirteen-piece band, and, since 1957, the simplicity that had prevailed in the studio during the early days had been succeeded by considerably more expansive arrangements.

Jules Bihari's strategy was to put B. B. King into more and more elaborate settings as his reputation and popularity grew. Obedient to the cliché that artistic maturity is synonymous with elaborate display, Bihari went along with show business logic, which insists that artists in the public eye must be accompanied by bands playing written-out arrangements that leave little room for improvisation. In token of B. B. King's arrival among the greats, he was put into the hands of one of the leading session musicians of the day, Maxwell Davis.

Davis had started out as a humble tenor saxophone player, and had made a name for himself as an accompanist, live and on record, for the cream of the California rhythm and blues scene, from Charles Brown and T-Bone Walker to Johnny Moore and the Three Blazers or Amos Milburn. His arrangement of the latter's famous number, "Chicken Shack Boogie," had made Davis a name to reckon with in the music business. Since the early fifties he had been a bandleader and arranger as well as a saxophonist, and was one of the most sought-after producers on the West Coast. It was natural for the Biharis to think of him in connection with their biggest artist. From 1957 onwards, Davis's trademarks were present on most of King's recordings. His strength lay in his ability to create an easily recognizable ensemble sound that could also be subtly adapted to the personality of each artist it accompanied. In King's case, this was all the easier because the musicians who worked with him on stage also came into the studio, directed by Davis and playing his scores. Another of his trademarks was the prominence given to sax players in the Coleman Hawkins mold, who always found a way to slip in a rasping solo between two verses.

Maxwell Davis's big band productions gave B. B. King no cause for complaint—far from it. He had always had a fondness for the swing ensembles he had heard on the radio as a child. In addition, he saw the use of brass on his records as proof that he had achieved not just musical goals, but social ones, too. As he explained to musicologist Arnold Shaw: "After the big band era, blues singers started being accompanied by horns and rhythm groups instead of just guitar and harp. But the reason that this happened was because, before that, the blues singers just could not afford to be backed by bands. . . . When you went to one of these [music] stores, you had to pay cash. They didn't know you, and you didn't have any credit. At that time, a horn was costing like a hundred dollars. Gosh, in those days, it would take me five months to make a hundred dollars. . . . So you bought whatever instrument you could afford—and that was the guitar."[33]

By the end of the fifties, things had changed. If he was not to be overshadowed by singers like Brook Benton and Jackie Wilson, B. B. King had to lead a big band at his shows; otherwise African-Americans would see him as a backward-looking figure playing old-fashioned music. "I think this big band was a kind of smart thing I did, if I ever did anything that was smart," King remarks. "Rock 'n' roll had come in at the time and people weren't digging the blues singers so much. But by having a big band, I was able to play behind many of the rock stars like Jackie Wilson, Sam Cooke and others. I could go into jazz clubs with the sound. The band would play a set and then I would come on as featured guitarist with my group."[34]

One of King's most important memories from these years is the series of recordings he made with the most famous big bands. "I did sides with Dorsey and Ellington," he later said with pride. "The Biharis had bought the rights to a group of masters. Instead of calling in another singer, they had me dub in vocals on the band tracks. In fact, we did 'Yes Indeed' with Tommy Dorsey. I used to keep copies of these records under lock and key—because people would never believe that B. B. King had recorded with Ellington, Basie, and Dorsey."[35]

In fact, Ellington, Basie and Dorsey did not appear on these records; the album sleeves gave the impression that they were present on what were actually versions of their best-known numbers, played by some of their musicians and arranged by Maxwell Davis. To say this is not to detract from King's abilities; he was fully on top of the situation, and proved himself to be a more than merely competent jazz singer. His interpretation of "Every Day I Have the Blues" with Basie's musicians is especially interesting, since it can be compared with the version he had made five years before. While the phrasing and diction on his 1955 hit are clearly indebted to the gospel-influenced side of R&B, the big band version spotlights a B. B. who is a successful jazz singer with a compelling sense of swing.

As the new decade dawned, B. B. King was obviously aiming for a more and more sophisticated sound, without turning his back on his blues origins. In professional terms, at thirty-five he was an artist who had achieved everything he had set out to do, and one who had been made a major star thanks to his relationship with the Bihari brothers. Despite a number of disappointing records, his time with Modern is the foundation on which King's career has rested, even down to the present day. "Three O' Clock Blues," "You Know I Love You," "Woke Up This Morning," "Sweet Little Angel," "Every Day," "Sweet Sixteen," "You Done Lost Your Good Thing" and " I Need You So Bad" have been central to his repertoire for more than thirty years. In addition, he became a master of his instrument and expert in leading a band during this vital period of musical and personal development.

It's not surprising that King's private life suffered as a result of his constant musical activity. Since his separation from Martha, he had had no chance to start another family, although he continued to make new female acquaintances at a frenetic pace. The media several times reported romantic attachments, and once even a marriage: in January 1956, a short item in *Billboard* stated that King was about to marry Dorothy Anderson, a young and good-looking dancer he had met while touring in Florida. That was a matter of rumor and exaggeration rather than reality, but King was a young, attractive and wealthy artist who provoked admiration and excitement in the female half of his audience. It's well known that popular singers usually find most of their fans among women; it is they who buy singles, and drag their boyfriends to the clubs and concert halls where their favorite stars are appearing.

B. B. King has never been one to withstand the ardor of his groupies, and after a few years found himself the putative father of a swarm of children, born to different mothers in various parts of the United States. Living as he does by a firm moral code, he has never tried to dodge his responsibilities in this or any other area of life, even though it can be difficult for a musician to know if a child is really his. "When a lady says the baby is yours, the only question to ask is 'Was you in there?' If the answer is yes, then it's yours."[36] For B. B. King, himself an orphan, it was unthinkable to abandon a child, whatever its origins.

This fundamental acceptance of the importance of the family was proof that King wanted ultimately to find emotional stability with a wife who would understand him, especially one who would accept his way of life. One of his best-sellers in 1957, "I Want to Get Married" set matters out clearly: "I want to get married, but no woman will hear my plea / Yes it just seems somehow, I can't get one to walk down the aisle with me." This was a prophetic song; a year later, in June 1958, King would be married to his second wife, Sue Carol Hall, in the Gotham Hotel in Detroit by his friend Reverend C. L. Franklin—Aretha's father.

In a mid-fifties magazine for girls, B. B. King described what he was looking for in an ideal companion: "I don't dig these chicks who think they know it all. Man, have you ever been tied up with something you thought was fine at the beginning of the evening and later ended up as a drag. That's right, Prez, it ain't necessary for any gal to have all the answers, especially when there isn't a person on the face of this whole world who knows everything. I like a gal to be well mannered, fairly attractive (not beautiful, mind ya'), have a cool sense of humor and, most of all she must not be a 'know-it-all.' "[37]

The new Mrs. King fitted this description in all respects. Like him she was from Indianola, where her mother owned the Club Ebony. At the age of eighteen, Sue King was a pretty and exceptionally intelligent young woman; she had been to college, which was unusual for an African-American woman in the South of those days. At first, King and his wife toured together so as not to be parted, but this set-up couldn't last, mainly because Sue already had a child from before her marriage, which made it difficult to sustain such an unstable way of life. In an effort to solve this problem, B. B. King realized one of his oldest dreams, and bought a house in the Los Angeles suburb of South Pasadena, California, not far from where his own father had moved shortly before with his family.

For a rootless person like him, owning a home symbolized both social success and a happy family life. Since his divorce from Martha, he had been content to live in apartments in Memphis, spending his money on clothes, instruments and transport for his band, not to mention indulging his passion for gambling. With the Los Angeles house, he was finally allowing himself to think of his own needs, and giving tangible shape to his rise in the world; in ten years, an orphaned farm worker from Mississippi had determinedly become famous, made a career for himself, and started a family. He seemed unstoppable.

4

THE YEARS OF UNCERTAINTY
(1961-1966)

Had he known them, the B. B. King of the early sixties might have appreciated the words of the English adventurer and poet Sir Walter Raleigh: "Fain would I climb, yet fear I to fall." In fact, it would be wrong to speak of a downfall in King's case, for there was no artistic failure, nor was he forgotten by the public. In the harsh world of show business, however, not to go forward is to go backward, and it was a decline of this kind, gentler but ultimately just as cruel, that B. B. King experienced. Accordingly, it's slightly artificial to draw a dividing line in his career at the start of the sixties, but it cannot be denied that from 1960 onwards, King's career was becoming humdrum after ten years of success, and was progressively losing the luster that had set him apart from the rest until then. Actually this was not due to an erosion of King's talents, but simply to the fact that this was a period of commercial decline for blues music in general in the Afro-American community.

The best indicator of this slow falling off is the gradual decline of his chart success. In both *Cash Box* and *Billboard* his name was becoming less prominent with each passing month, as his records ceased to figure in the Top Ten of the rhythm and blues charts, and became stuck in obscurity at the foot of the list. From "Three O'Clock Blues" in 1951 to "Walkin' Dr. Bill" in 1960, King had notched up a record-breaking twenty-four hits, eighteen of which reached the *Billboard* Top Ten. A comparison with the next decade speaks for itself: King's records still sold steadily, but without the dazzling success of his early years. He had twenty-eight entries in the *Billboard* charts between 1961 and 1970—four more than during the previous ten years, in fact—but only five of them reached the Top Ten, and not one made it to the top of the R&B hit parade. It was the same story in *Cash Box*: thirty-five chart entries, but only four really big sellers. Finally, whereas in the fifties his big hits had stayed on the charts for ten, twelve, and fifteen weeks—even eighteen weeks in the case of 1952's "You Know I Love You"—after 1960 they seldom appeared for more than five or six weeks.

The trade papers' charts are no more than a weathervane, but they do show the way the wind is blowing, and were a measure of the way King's career was going into the doldrums. Record sales are a vital aspect of a musician's career. Before World War II, a musician in a specialized area like blues could consider him- or herself a successful artist without being a recording star, but with the arrival of radio programming directed at African-American listeners, and the growth of large numbers of independent record companies, there was no success without hit records.

By the time America entered the war in 1941, more than half the records produced were being sold to jukebox operators rather than to private customers. The use of records in radio broadcasting, instead of the live orchestras that had featured before, was to revolutionize the market, stimulating an unprecedented demand for discs. Every factor seemed to favor this development: new technology was cutting recording and production costs. It was also reducing the price of radios and record players; the steady rise in African-American living standards since the early forties had enabled more black households to acquire them, and had led to a considerable rise in record sales.

It was in this context that *Billboard* had launched its "Harlem Hit Parade" in October 1942, to chronicle black record sales as accurately as possible, at first in the northeastern states, but soon all over the country. After several changes of name, the title "Best Selling Retail Rhythm & Blues Records" was settled on in June 1949, emphasizing that the aim was to list the top sellers, and incidentally launching the term "rhythm & blues." "Soul" and "black" have succeeded "rhythm and blues" as favored descriptions of the music, but sales figures have remained the bottom line where the hit parade is concerned.

Record sales, therefore, have defined the financial health of a musician like B. B. King right from the start. On release, records are made into hits or not largely by the disc jockeys at the larger African-American radio stations in the main urban centers. The amount of airplay received is usually a primary factor in generating approval for tunes, and consequently record sales as well as concert attendance, among the listening audience. In the early sixties, changes both in musical styles and in listeners' tastes meant that blues singers were in for a rough ride. The most popular ones survived, but they often had to sweeten their music, as in the cases of Junior Parker and Bobby "Blue" Bland, whose record company significantly dropped the "Blue" from his name. As for King, the radio presenters respected his work, and both he and his record company kept in close touch with them; as a result, they still programmed his new releases, but with less enthusiasm, as the likes of Brook Benton, James Brown and Jackie Wilson became the hot names.

Sales of B. B.'s singles were adversely affected by these changes. To counter this, the Bihari brothers out in California tried a new policy, with the aim of maximizing the profit to be made from their biggest star. In the early fifties, two giants of recording and radio, RCA Victor and Columbia, had been at loggerheads; out of the contest had come two microgroove recording standards. In 1948, at the height of the battle over the replacement for the fragile and low-fidelity 78 rpm record, Columbia tried to beat off RCA's new 45 rpm system with a 33 rpm disc. The long-playing 33 rpm format was ideal for classical music, but RCA won the day in the popular market, where the 45 rpm single became the universal successor to the 78. Forty-fives were much better suited to radio and jukeboxes alike, and their low price meant that youngsters preferred them.

The 33 rpm LP took longer to establish itself, but its hour came in the late fifties. The children of the average American family were buying the hits of the day on singles; their parents, however, were ready to stand the expense of acquiring LPs to play on their impressive record players. With their longer playing time, these provided much more music, at a cost per minute that was actually less than that of a single. At Modern, the bosses were well aware of this trend, and in 1958 they started to release albums by B. B. King on their subsidiary label, Crown, the name of which may have been a tribute to their king of the blues.

B. B.'s early Crown LPs, like Singing the Blues (Crown 5020) and The Blues (Crown 5063) were compilations of his greatest hits. Later, purposely recorded albums would appear on Crown and Kent, consisting of the current single, plus some less impressive titles recorded specifically for the LP market. In 1960, King cut a record with a gospel group, The Charioteers, which is strikingly representative of this new approach.

In this unusual context, King was going back to his religious roots with a dozen of the best-known spirituals, like "Ole Time Religion" and "Swing Low Sweet Chariot." According to King, he wanted to pay a tribute to an aunt of his, a fervent Christian who had never let him sing the blues in her house when he was a youngster. More to the point, Modern and the Biharis were trying to widen his audience.

Another try at this, in a very different vein, happened when King was asked to record a set of instrumentals, featuring his guitar backed by a full orchestra. The craze for rock 'n' roll dances like the twist, the mashed potato and the popeye was at its height, and Modern was hoping that this change of direction would appeal to white adolescents, and be a foot in the door of middle America. Aside from a single on Kent, which made few waves in the surf music era, these instrumentals were to stay on the shelves at Modern until the British firm Ace acquired the rights, and issued them in 1985.

Given these setbacks for the Biharis, B. B. King was reluctant to renew his contract with the California company, for he found much to object to in their policy on albums. In particular, he took offense when Modern sold his LPs on their Crown subsidiary at the bargain basement price of ninety-nine cents. Apart from the fact that his royalties were reduced accordingly, King felt that selling his music at a discount was bad for his image. He had hesitated in continuing his relationship with Modern in 1959; now he decided to look seriously at making a deal with someone else when his contract came up for renewal in 1962.

As the deadline approached, he considered several options. As before, the Chess brothers in Chicago were in the running. Their offer seemed tempting, for they had a number of popular performers in their catalog, among them the black rock 'n' roll stars Chuck Berry and Bo Diddley, whose music had contributed to the decline of King's popularity. Joining the Chess stable would ensure that King was working for a label that knew how to adapt to changing fashions, unlike Modern, which had missed the rock 'n' roll bandwagon.

At that time, Willie Dixon was combining the jobs of producer, lyricist and composer for the Chess brothers, but he still tried to persuade King not to get involved with them, believing, rightly or wrongly, that Leonard and Phil Chess were unfairly exploiting their artists: "B. B. King once asked me about coming to Chess in the early 1960s when him and Chess were just about to get together. I told B. B., 'Look, you'd be doing the wrong thing if you worked for Chess,' and he didn't get with him. I don't know whether I was the cause of it but I knew damn well what Chess was doing to everybody else. Why the hell should you get on the same boat?"[1]

Dixon's opinion wasn't the only factor affecting B. B.'s judgment when it came to making a decision. King had also asked for the expert advice of his idol Louis Jordan, who told him that, unlike smaller firms, major companies treated their artists fairly, at least as far as royalty payments were concerned. Besides, Chess wasn't the only company taking an interest, for B. B.'s sales at the time were far from negligible. The eventual winner was ABC. Where Modern, Chess or Peacock were independents, ABC was a "major," in the jargon of the record industry, and one of a select band of half a dozen labels that operated on an international scale, among them Columbia, RCA Victor and Mercury.

ABC had started life as one of the three big broadcasting networks which dominated radio and television in the United States. Since its founding in 1943, ABC had failed to make up for its late start, and had not caught up with the other two networks, CBS and NBC, in either audience figures or turnover. ABC's management decided that diversification was one of the answers to this problem; as a first step the firm had merged with Paramount Pictures in 1955, with a view to streamlining the production of programs needed to feed the company's TV stations. The same year, the radio side of the business took a similar step by launching its own record company, ABC-Paramount. Working out of a prestigious office on Broadway in New York, ABC-Paramount intended to concentrate chiefly on pop music, but also to issue children's records, jazz, and rhythm and blues.

Samuel Clark, president of ABC-Paramount, had become aware of the latter area of music in 1957, following the unexpected success of several white singers with African-American record buyers. In the space of a few months, Paul Anka, Danny and the Juniors, and the Royal Teens had had hits in the *Billboard* R&B charts. The same year saw further confirmation of the commercial potential of R&B, this time from an African-American artist, Lloyd Price. Price was from New Orleans, and was one of a number of black musicians whose sound was easily accepted by white audiences looking for just a hint of the exotic. Price's movement towards this new audience is very obvious when "Just Because," his first hit for ABC-Paramount in March 1957, is compared to the very watered-down sound of "Personality," two years later.

ABC-Paramount's next recruit was Ray Charles; in 1960 he left Atlantic and his no-holds-barred rhythm and blues sound, defecting to the heart of middle America, as was shown above all by his country-and-western output. In Chicago, the burgeoning sound of soul music supplied ABC with one of its greatest creators when Curtis Mayfield and his group, the Impressions, joined Samuel Clark's roster in 1961, bringing with them a series of superbly polished compositions, "Gypsy Woman" and "People Get Ready" among them.

In 1962, ABC-Paramount's management decided to consolidate their position in the R&B market. So it was that Fats Domino and B. B. King left Imperial and Modern respectively, and signed with ABC. "I had talked to Fats Domino," King remembers. "He was with them—and he told me that they would like to have me. And he went on to tell me, if you're going to be recognized in the record business you have to at least have a company that is recognized. Like if you've sold a million copies of a record or an album, it should be certified. And as we were [with the Biharis] it would never be. And he was quite right, because we sold many, many records. But I never did see any certifications, even though I had two or three gold records that they gave me. But I never saw anything that was legitimately documented. So I went to ABC."[2]

The break with Modern went smoothly, although King missed the quasi-family relationship he had had with the Bihari brothers since joining RPM in 1950. He had a genuine friendship with Saul, Joe and Jules Bihari; on the other hand, their policy of selling his music on cut-price albums, at a time when the single was king of the airwaves, could only hurt his career. Leaving Modern in no way diminished his affection for Jules especially. "Jules Bihari passed, and I'm sorry I didn't know about it until it had happened, and I wasn't able to go to his funeral. I'm saying that because I loved the guy; he was to me, one of the greatest people in the record business. He is one of the people that knew about recording black music. And because, what he would usually do is allow you to be yourself; do your own thing; the way you feel like doing it. All he did was try to keep the technical parts of it right. And I think one record's best when you're able to do that."[3]

By all accounts, the atmosphere in ABC-Paramount's New York office was very different, and much more formal. In financial terms, however, B. B. King was better off than he could ever have been at a smaller company like Modern; he received the tidy sum of twenty-five thousand dollars as an advance on signing his new contract. Apart from the financial side, though, the new deal wasn't as stunning as it might have looked. In particular, ABC's producers had only a vague knowledge of R&B and of the expectations of King's core audience. It turned out that ABC's intentions were the same as the Biharis' had been during the latter days at Modern; the aim was to remodel B. B. King's image, and try to break him into the less specialized and more lucrative pop market, with the initial emphasis on albums.

His first session for ABC took place on 1 March 1962 in Los Angeles. King wasn't too far out of his element, since these recordings were supervised by Maxwell Davis. The big change came the following September, when ABC-Paramount's in-house staff producers decided to sweeten King's blues by mixing it with a large orchestra, under the direction of Belford Kendricks: "They started to think in terms of B. B. King becoming a major force in the music business," he says. "But not so much as the blues singer and blues guitarist as he had been. I remember the first session: we had 18 strings! They had voices! Now that's frightening!"[4]

In terms of repertoire, this policy meant abandoning the slow blues and shuffles that had always been King's stock-in-trade. In their place, ABC's producers selected ballads like "Guess Who," which had been a hit for the black crooner Jesse Belvin in spring 1959. In April 1963, ABC and King maintained the new direction, this time with Teacho Wiltshire's orchestra and kitsch compositions like "Young Dreamers" and "How Do I Love You."

The results were not long in coming. In a few months, King disappeared from the hit parades almost entirely, losing his bedrock African-American audience without winning over white purchasers as compensation. After a disastrous 1963, 1964 brought three very modest hits on ABC-Paramount, with the best-selling of them, "Never Trust a Woman" going no higher than number ninety in the *Billboard* charts. One of them, "Help the Poor," was only on the hit parade for two weeks, which comes as no surprise when one listens in disbelief to the maracas, congas, and assorted percussion used in an attempt to give this Cuban-style blues an overlay of exotic tone colors.

The only respite from the stagnation was "How Blue Can You Get," a number borrowed from B. B.'s friend Louis Jordan. This song stood out, thanks to the relative simplicity of its arrangement, and the caustic humor of the lyrics, which have made it one of King's standbys in live performance ever since: "I gave you a brand new Ford, but you said, 'I want a Cadillac' / I bought you a ten-dollar dinner and you said, 'Thanks for the snack' / I let you live in my penthouse, you said it was just a shack / I gave you seven children, and now you wanna give 'em back."

Almost everything else in King's studio work for ABC was ill directed, and depressed his career still further. It didn't help that the Biharis were still using Kent to release the many unissued sides that King had cut before leaving them. Ironically, by doing so they enabled King to maintain a presence in the singles market; from 1962 to 1967 Kent scored no fewer than nine smallish hits with him, while ABC had only four. The final Kent single to show up on the hit parade was "That Evil Child," one of the last titles King had recorded for the Biharis, in 1961; it made the *Billboard* soul charts early in spring 1971! In artistic terms, this phenomenon engendered a certain amount of confusion which was unhelpful to King. While ABC was doing its utmost to give him an image in keeping with the new decade, the release of sides that were more than ten years old—like 1966's "I Stay in the Mood," cut at a 1957 session—made it seem that King's music was dated and passé.

ABC-Paramount' s bosses now began to ask themselves some serious questions about how they should steer King's recording career. Kent was selling more singles with very traditional numbers like "Rock Me Baby" (adapted from Arthur Crudup's popular 1945 version of an old theme), "Eyesight to the Blind" (an old number of Rice "Sonny Boy Williamson" Miller's) and "Blue Shadows" (a hit for Lowell Fulson in 1950) than ABC was with the overproduced ballads they were giving B. B. to sing. This evidently gave pause for thought. Finally, in late 1964, ABC realized that

King was not about to become another Frank Sinatra or Billy Eckstine, and that his talent would only blossom fully when he was performing the carefully crafted rhythm and blues that was his trademark.

From this time onwards, the change of direction is very obvious. In June 1965, accompanied by his own musicians, King cut an album of old blues standards like "See See Rider," "Goin' to Chicago Blues," "Cherry Red" and "How Long How Long Blues." This was a long way from the sentimental angle of his previous efforts, although the jazzy arrangements, recalling the swinging R&B of the immediate postwar years, propelled King into a musical world closer to that of blues shouters like Big Joe Turner and Jimmy Rushing than to his own up-to-date style.

Only in 1966, with a definite return to the urban blues, did King manage to regain the highest reaches of record sales. The song that carried him to number two on the *Billboard* charts and number three in *Cash Box* was called "Don't Answer the Door." Composed by saxophonist Jimmy Johnson, this song fitted ideally with his stage image as an urbane bluesman, macho but pleasant at the same time. Two years before on "How Blue Can You Get," King had played a man being pushed around by a troublesome girlfriend; this time, albeit with humor, he was displaying pathological jealousy, tyrannizing his woman and refusing to let her have any visitors: "You might feel a little sick, baby, and you know you're home all alone / I don't want the doctor at my house, so you just suffer, suffer, suffer 'til I get home / I don't want a soul, woman, hangin' around my house when I'm not at home / I don't want you to answer the door for nobody, baby, when you're home and you know you're all alone."

For B. B., the success of "Don't Answer the Door" was not an unmixed blessing. Obviously, he was pleased to have found renewed favor with his audience after a long period in the wilderness. For an artist such as he, a best-selling record was as good for his fortune as for his fame. Nevertheless, although African-Americans loved "Don't Answer the Door," it was quite another story with the huge white American audience, which continued to ignore him completely. It's one thing to be a star in the eyes of black America, but quite another to be known and admired by everyone else—by 90 percent of Americans, in other words.

Once again, the hit parade is informative: when "Don't Answer the Door" was number two in the *Billboard* R&B charts, it was only a disappointing seventy-two in the same magazine's Hot 100, which listed national sales in all musical categories lumped together. "Records are funny," said B. B. "You aim them for the colored market, then suddenly the white folks like them and wham! you've got both markets plus whites at your dances. That's what happened to Fats Domino. . . .

But we don't play rock and roll. Our music is the blues straight from the Delta. I believe we'll make it on that."[5]

This was a time when Berry Gordy at Tamla-Motown was finally "crossing over" by making white America take note of African-American artists like the Four Tops, the Temptations and Diana Ross and the Supremes. For B. B. King, "Don't Answer the Door" was proof that he had failed his entrance examination into the closed world of white show business. Never one to deny his origins, he had been doing everything he could to enlarge the scope of his music since the start of the sixties. Leaving Modern for ABC-Paramount was evidently part of a plan, of which the next step was to change his management: in 1962, he left Evelyn Johnson's Houston-based Buffalo Booking Agency to join the Milt Shaw Booking Agency in New York, one of the biggest in the country.

From a financial angle, King had no cause for complaint about his new agents, for the jobs he got were often better paid than the ones he had been doing on the chitlin circuit hitherto. But there was a heavy price to pay for the extra money. Instead of topping the bill, he was asked to play as a support act, as he had once done for Tiny Bradshaw; now, his band accompanied the new stars of rock 'n' roll and soul like Sam Cooke and Lloyd Price, and his own role was to warm up the audience at the start of the show.

For teenagers who had come to hear Cooke and Price doing their dance hits, King's slice-of-life stories for grownups were far from welcome, and they got at best a mixed reception; sometimes they got booing and catcalls. B. B. King has a bitter memory from those frustrating times: "They said, 'Now we bring you B. B. King,' and everybody said, 'Boo!' Well, that hurt me very deeply. I remember thinking to myself—I did a tune called 'Sweet Sixteen,' which is one of my big tunes, and there's a few lines in there that kind of pleased me, like getting it off my chest: 'Treat me mean, but I'll keep on loving you just the same / But one of these days you'll give a lot of money, just to hear somebody call my name.' That kind of made me feel better. And believe it or not, I could hear silence over the audience when I sang that."[6]

To put it in perspective, the audiences that booed the first notes of "Sweet Sixteen," "Three O'Clock Blues" or "How Blue Can You Get" were not turning against B. B. King so much as against the blues itself. Since the war, African-American musical tastes had changed considerably. In the latter half of the fifties, there had been an initial upheaval, with the arrival of rock 'n' roll, a marriage between rough Delta R&B and hillbilly music that had given rise to the exuberant sounds of Fats Domino and Lloyd Price. At the end of the decade, soul music, born from the intense emotions of gospel, had won the allegiance of most young African-Americans, who saw their own feelings reflected in the carefree joie de vivre of Sam Cooke's "Twistin' the Night Away" and "Having a Party," the adolescent sentimentality of ballads like Smokey Robinson and the Miracles' "You've Really Got a Hold on Me," and, a few years later, the racial pride proclaimed by James Brown's "Say It Loud—I'm Black and I'm Proud."

B. B. King's music, on the other hand, reminded listeners of everything that seemed painful and humiliating in the black experience. In his blues, King didn't sing about romance, but about love that was lost or unattainable; his words and his imagery referred constantly to life in the South or the ghetto, realities his audience wanted to escape. Despite his problems, King refused to abandon the idiom that had inspired him since childhood, and had been the vehicle of his rise to fame. It hurt him to realize that his lifelong heroes were often seen as dirty and illiterate, and he decided to fight for the blues. Perhaps the hardest thing was that it was African-Americans who were quickest to bad-mouth the blues, no doubt because they thought it a regressive music. "You feel very bad when someone criticizes it. Maybe some people don't want to be reminded that it happened to them, too."[7]

In the mid-sixties, the sense of shame that some adults felt about the blues they had grown up with had spread to most of the youngsters who attended the marathon concerts given at theaters like the Royal in Philadelphia and the Apollo in the heart of Harlem, still shrines to black music. The problem was so acute that concert promoters were becoming reluctant to book artists who had filled their venues through the previous decade.

Bobby Schiffman, manager of the Apollo at that time, had been forced to ask himself some searching questions. "I had a blues show at the theatre. B. B. King, Bobby 'Blue' Bland, T-Bone Walker, Jimmy Witherspoon, Sonny Terry and Brownie McGhee, and Odetta. The show did very poorly, so I called the cast up to my office on Tuesday and said, 'Hey, let's sit down and bullshit. I want to find out why the show didn't do well, and I want your opinions.' So we sat in my office, and I sent out for coffee and doughnuts and bourbon, and we sat for a couple of hours and talked. . . . I'll tell you why that show did poorly, as exposed by that discussion. Blues represented, at that time, misery. Misery and blues were a throwback to slavery, to a time when the Black man, intellectually, was at the lowest point in his history. And Black folks from the street didn't want to hear that shit. They came to the theatre to be uplifted, to see the glamour of four-hundred-dollar mohair suits. To see the glamour of the gorgeous gowns, and the hairdos, and the beautiful makeup, and the magnificent sets. The glamour of it all took them away from their own troubles. They didn't want to reminisce or reflect on the troubles that were proposed by the blues. For that reason the blues were never a significantly popular attraction at the Apollo."[8]

If rejection by young audiences was a recent phenomenon, hostility to the blues was no new thing. Many religious people considered it to be the devil's music, and a considerable part of the African-American intelligentsia was scornful, seeing it only as a reminder of a bygone age and symptomatic of a deplorable submissiveness in the face of white power. For a substantial part of the black middle class, in the time of Dr. King and Malcolm X, blues was Uncle Tom music.

If King had always been held in high esteem by musicians like Dizzy Gillespie and Miles Davis—both of whom were actually friends—jazz amateurs did a good deal to perpetuate this myth, the more so because they scorned the commercial success of blues and R&B. In the mid-sixties, B. B. King told the sociologist Charles Keil about the sneering response of the jazz world when blues was mentioned: "When I go to a jazz club, sometimes the leader or the MC will say 'B. B. King, the well-known blues singer, is in the audience tonight,' and the way he says 'blues' you know he really means 'nasty.' . . . When a lot of people say 'blues singer', they're thinking of some ignorant lush moaning in a gutter some place. . . . There's no reason why a man can't sing the blues as a profession and still be a gentleman. That's the main reason I'm sticking with blues because I'd like to show people that it can be done."[9]

If King was having problems with many in his African-American audience, perhaps there was hope to be found in the educated whites who were taking an increasing interest in the blues. For some years now, there had been a growing awareness of the riches of black culture, at first among New York intellectuals, then on university campuses. In Greenwich Village, in Cambridge, Massachusetts, in Chicago, Los Angeles and San Francisco and at the Newport Jazz Festival, the blues was attracting considerable attention in the person of artists like Lightnin' Hopkins, Josh White, and Sonny Terry and Brownie McGhee. But while Bukka White's colorful performances were acclaimed by white student audiences, "Cousin B" was rejected by them out of hand, as a traitor to his roots who had corrupted the pure acoustic "country blues" by plugging it into an amplifier. These contrasting opinions were made flesh in December 1963, when White's and King's paths crossed on the West Coast. At the same time that Bukka was playing for enthusiastic students in folklore classes at the University of California at Berkeley, his cousin was appearing at Sweet's Ballroom, a club in the Oakland ghetto, before an exclusively black audience.[10]

Some artists had got the message, and adjusted their acts according to the audience; John Lee Hooker was one. In the Detroit ghetto, he wore a spangled suit and was backed by a rhythm section in the very clubs where he had started out in the late forties, but in Europe, at Newport, or on the Harvard campus, he came on stage in jeans and workshirt, with just an acoustic guitar and a set of mannered so-called folk-blues.

B. B. King was in no position to change that easily. His band's complex arrangements, the integral part played by a full rhythm section, even his personal sophistication, wouldn't let him pass himself off to young America as a Delta blues singer just up from the plantation. His only outlet seemed to be the people he had emerged from, working-class African-Americans. Thanks to his proud and purist attitude, and his refusal to abandon his own brand of blues in order to slide into soul music like Bobby Bland, King was in an unique position in the American entertainment world. In 1966, Charles Keil summed it up neatly in his fine study of urban blues: "B. B. King is the only straight blues singer in America with a large, adult, nation-wide, and almost entirely Negro audience. If the adjectives 'unique,' 'pure,' and 'authentic' apply to any blues singer alive today, they certainly apply to B. B. King."[11]

After several years of trial and error, ABC-Paramount finally succumbed to the evidence, and King's two most outstanding albums up to 1967 were undoubtedly *Blues Is King* and *Live at the Regal*, both recorded live in Chicago in the ideal setting of large ghetto venues. These two concert albums bear witness to the hard times he was going through; the thirteen-piece band that had backed King in the fifties had been drastically slimmed down. King's voice and guitar were supported only by Duke Jethro on organ, his long-serving drummer Sonny Freeman, a bassist, a trumpeter, and one or two tenor saxophones. As for his audience, the reactions heard on these two albums are proof that they were more enthusiastic than ever.

It is worth spending some time to consider *Live at the Regal* in detail, for it is a monumental example of King's art, and, in the opinion of most of his fans, even today the greatest testament to his genius. It is exceptional precisely because it preserves a typical King concert from those days; its contents are at once extraordinary and the norm.

The Regal stood in the heart of Chicago's South Side, on the corner of two of the ghetto's main arteries, Parkway and 47th Street. This enormous theater, elaborately decorated in Moorish stucco, had been built during the prosperous years after World War I. Long before B. B. King, James Brown, and Gladys Knight appeared there, the Regal had welcomed vaudeville artists like Bessie Smith and

1. Riley "B. B." King, WDIA portrait, Memphis, early 1950s.

2. WDIA on-air personalities, from left to right, Joe Hill Louis, A. C. Williams, Ford Nelson, B. B. King, Hot Rod Hulbert, Nat D. Williams. Memphis, early 1950s.

4. B. B. King, studio portrait. Memphis, early 1950s.

3. WDIA on-air personalities, from left to right, Joe Hill Louis, B. B. King, Starr McKinney, Ford Nelson, Rufus Thomas, Willa Monroe, and Nat D. Williams. Memphis, early 1950s.

5.

6. Backstage gathering in Memphis, early 1950s with Johnny Ace, B. B. King, Bonita Cole, Bill Harvey, and Big Mama Thornton.

7. B. B. King with Evelyn Young and Bill Harvey and his orchestra. Club Handy, Beale Street, Memphis, early 1950s.

8. B. B. King with A. C. "Moohaw the Deejay" Williams at a club date. Memphis, mid-1950s.

9. B. B. King and Orchestra. Memphis, mid-1950s.

10. B. B. King and Orchestra. Jazz great George Coleman, right. Memphis, 1955.

11. B. B. King with first road crew, band, and "Big Red," the jalopy bus. In front of Club Handy, Beale Street, Memphis, circa 1955. From left to right: B. B. King, Shinny Walker, Venita Cole, Earl Forest, Evelyn Young, Cato Walker, "Sleepy," Jerry Smith, Ted Curry, Millard Lee, Floyd Newman, Kenny Sands, Calvin Owens, Richard Lillie, Lawrence Birdeye, Paul Pinkman, and Frank Brown.

12. B. B. King and Ray Charles, backstage meeting. Memphis, mid-1950s.

13. B. B. King and Duke Ellington.

14. B. B. King with Elvis Presley and unidentified female. Ellis auditorium, Memphis, mid-1950s.

15.

16. B. B. King and
Orchestra with
Honeymoon Garner,
organ. Club
Paradise, Memphis,
June 6, 1965.

17. B. B. King at the Newport Jazz Festival, 1969.

19. B. B. King in concert, mid-1970s.

18. B. B. King relaxing, mid-1970s.

20-23. B. B. King in his New York apartment, mid-1970s.

21.

22.

23.

24-27. B. B. King in concert, Montreal, Canada, 1978.

25.

27.

28. B. B. King entertaining students at Yale University, mid-1970s.

29. B. B. King receiving honorary doctorate, Yale University, 1977.

30. B. B. King, Albert King, and Bobby "Blue" Bland reminiscing in San Francisco, 1993.

31.

32. B. B. King performing with Emmy Lou Harris, Lyle Lovett and Bonnie Raitt at Willie Nelson's 60th birthday concert, Austin, Texas, October 23, 1993.

33. Russian promotional poster featuring B. B. King, 1979.

right: 34. Program for B. B. King's performance at Parchman State Penitentiary.

35. B. B. King's Blues Club and Restaurant, Beale Street, Memphis.

36. B. B. King's Blues Club and Restaurant menu.

37. B. B. King Road, Indianola, Mississippi.

38. Hand and foot prints in sidewalk, Church Street, Indianola, Mississippi, made June 5, 1980.

39. B. B. King's Homecoming concert, Indianola, Mississippi, June 5, 1989, filmed by the BBC (camera, right).

40.

41. B. B. King's Homecoming concert, Indianola, Mississippi, May 30, 1997.

42. B. B. King's Homecoming concert, Indianola, Mississippi, May 30, 1997.

43. B. B. King speaking at John Lee Hooker Achievement Award program, Blues Foundation, Memphis, November 1996.

44. B. B. King at the Medgar Evers Homecoming, Fayette, Mississippi, June, 1986.

Ida Cox; in the thirties, the greatest big bands of the swing era had appeared, led by Duke Ellington, Count Basie and Cab Calloway. The Regal always kept in touch with changing tastes and fashions, whether in music or movies; as Marlon Brando and James Dean replaced Clark Gable on the screen, so Aretha Franklin and Curtis Mayfield trod the boards instead of Earl Hines and Ella Fitzgerald.

At the time of *Live at the Regal*, the theater was an entertainment factory, with no fewer than thirty-six full-time employees, working shifts from one o'clock to midnight. Over this period, the same show—usually a mixture of music and films—was presented four or five times, first as a matinée, then in the evening. The show by B. B. King that Johnny Pate, his regular producer, recorded took place on the evening of 21 November 1964; as might be expected, this was a Saturday, when the public would be ready to spend some of yesterday's pay packet at the end of a hard week. As well as his own musicians, King was backed by the Regal's house band, directed by trumpeter and swing era veteran King Kolax; his brass and reed sections added a sonorous panache that was perfectly suited to the majestic delivery of the king of the blues.

King was probably not the only artist on the bill, but it's a safe bet that he was at the top of it. It's easy to envisage the local comedian keeping the audience happy with the usual smutty stories about two-timing women and street pimps while the music stands are changed.

The ticket price on a Saturday night is too high for the poorest members of the working class, and it's likely that the South Side's lower-middle and middle class have come out tonight. There are no young faces in the audience, which consists entirely of people of B. B.'s own generation, the very ones who bought his first discs fifteen years ago: businessmen, skilled workmen, construction workers, foremen, and a good many flaunting clothes that speak of wealth of which nobody knows the source, although everyone is sure that it's either prostitution or gambling, since, along with preaching, these are about the only ways to make money in the black community, and the preachers' sermons have been too hostile to the blues for them to get away with going to see B. B. King perform. The women wear long dresses and patent leather shoes, the men pin-striped suits and highly polished footwear. It's cold outside, and the Windy City is living up to its name, hence the furs and the camel hair coats.

Backstage, a signal tells the comedian that everything is finally ready, and after one last joke sets everyone roaring with laughter, he gives way to Pervis Spann, one of the most popular disc jockeys on WVON, the local black radio station. As the curtain rises to show the band sitting quietly behind music stands decorated with the initials BBK, Spann takes the microphone: "Ladies and gentlemen, how about a nice warm round of applause to welcome the world's greatest blues singer, the king of the blues, B. B. King!" Sonny Freeman plays a roll on the snare drum, and the band breaks into the first bars of "Every Day I Have the Blues," which has been the opening number at all King's concerts since 1955. From the second chorus onwards, King's guitar rides over the band, and B. B. appears in the spotlight, singing, "Every day, every day I have the blues / When you see me worried, woman, it's you I hate to lose." Things are underway.

"Every Day I Have the Blues" has been taken at breakneck tempo, and King stops the song after less than two minutes. The applause and shouts of encouragement are still fairly restrained at this stage. Over gospel piano chords, King greets his audience, and announces his intention of going back to his roots, with "some of the real old blues! If we should happen to play one that you remember, let us know it by makin' some noise." The band stops abruptly, and King hits a long, very bluesy lick, as the women in the audience shout their approval. When King launches into the words of "Sweet Little Angel," the hysteria increases, and shouts of "Come on, baby!" and "Tell us, B.!" mingle with cries of pleasure and high-pitched whistling. After three verses, Lucille—King's guitar—takes over, and generates just as many unbridled responses as did its owner's words. Every word, every note, is known and expected by the audience, which awaits them with bated breath, the better to react as soon as they are heard.

King moves on to "It's My Own Fault" without a break, after making a few comments about lost love which evoke more boisterous responses: "Let's think about a guy that loses his girl. Oh, it happens, believe me!" "I know it!" shouts a man in the front row, making King guffaw. The orchestra keeps playing, but King Kolax subtly takes the key up a semitone, to keep the audience's attention. The guitar's tone becomes more biting, and occasional male voices shout "Yeah, baby!" and "Sing the blues!" in encouragement; meanwhile, the women are still addressing the singer as he starts on his most recent hit, "How Blue Can You Get." A series of breaks punctuates the litany of indignities that King's woman has put him through; as the last of them ends, all the women are out of their seats and yelling at once, and pandemonium reigns. Keeping up the supercharged atmosphere he has built in the last few minutes, King leads the band into "Please Love Me," a fast shuffle that was a number-one hit in 1953, before he leaves the stage in an ecstatic storm of female screams.

Side two of *Live at the Regal* was probably recorded at the final concert that November Saturday night, and it runs along almost the same lines, except that the radio presenter acting as master of ceremonies is now E. Rodney Jones. The music is the purest blues, but the electric atmosphere, and the strong latent sexuality, are exactly like those at a southern Pentecostal church service. Instead of the Holy Scriptures, "Reverend" King's gospel is one of peace in the home and reconciliation between man and wife. In this respect, the monologue with which he ends "Worry, Worry" is typical:

"I'd like to tell you a little story now. Ladies, if you got a man, husband, whatever you wanna call him, and he don't do exactly like you think he should, don't cut him 'cause you can't raise him over again, you know. Don't hurt him, treat him nice. And fellows, I wanna say to you, if you got a wife, a woman or whatever you wanna call her, and she don't do like you think she should, don't go upside her head. That don't do but one thing, that make her a little smarter and she won't let you catch her the next time. So all you do is talk to her softly, real sweet you know, and you tell her: 'I know you'll do better.'" Just as in church, the problems tackled are everyday ones, the language and the imagery come straight from the ghetto, and everyone recognizes his or her own situation.

Once the concert is over, the hall empties slowly, and a queue of women waits to meet King backstage, dragging their husbands along. On a night like this, the photographer who has the concession at the Regal will make a small fortune from taking pictures of King's female admirers with their idol. If a woman is on her own, King allows closer and more daring poses before signing the resulting Polaroid. The photographer slips it into a small cardboard frame which will have pride of place on the sideboard, next to the television and between the magazine pictures of John Kennedy and Martin Luther King, Jr. These are the texts and subtexts of *Live at the Regal*, all of them showing King's unmatched mastery of three instruments: his voice, his guitar, and his audience.

Unknown to white America, rejected by young African-Americans, and losing record sales as a result, King had no choice but to rely on audiences of the kind he found at the Regal, and across the country at the other main stops on the chitlin circuit. Quite apart from the frustrations of playing to a limited audience, the endless touring was wearing him out. It's one thing to play three hundred concerts a year at the age of thirty, when your career is on the up and up; it's quite another to be unable to slow down at forty, because there are still payments to make on the band bus, and no other source of income with which to cover one's responsibilities to the family and others. King was lucky that he had an exceptionally strong constitution, and especially that he could overcome his tiredness with a few hours sleep, usually snatched on the road.

To get an idea of the unbelievable comings and goings that King's wandering life entailed at this time, consider his itinerary just in November and December 1962. In thirty-five days, he played twenty-three concerts in as many different towns. Between Baton Rouge, Louisiana, on 21 November and Pueblo, Colorado, on 29 December, King and his band visited Texas, Arkansas, Oklahoma, Mississippi, Tennessee and Alabama, before heading back towards Colorado via Mississippi, Arkansas, Louisiana, Texas and New Mexico. In all, they traveled nearly seven thousand miles, in hops that varied from sixty to seven hundred and fifty miles.

"You can't imagine how it is, out here. You spend three nights in one hotel and learn that the door to the right goes to the toilet and the one on the left goes out into the corridor. Then you change cities, and the first night in the new hotel, you wake up standing in the corridor, not sure where you are or how you got there. As it turns out, you turned right heading for the toilet, more asleep than awake, and the directions in this hotel are reversed."[12]

Even worse than the tiredness were the domestic tensions created by all this traveling, which were often hard to defuse. Scattered across the United States as his children were, it wasn't easy for B. B. King to maintain relationships with them, and the fact that he couldn't easily take part in their upbringing made him feel guilty, the more so because he himself had not been raised by his natural parents. "Like, I took my son to see Billie Holiday, Diana Ross in *Lady Sings the Blues*. And my son came back and said: 'Dad, did Billie Holiday really go through drugs like that?' I said, 'Well, yeah!' I almost cried, because I felt that I had really neglected to teach him certain things that I have preached to other people and didn't even take it home."[13]

One reason King was seeing less of his children was that since his remarriage he was trying to get home as often as possible, so as not to feel that he was neglecting his wife. Since buying their house in California in 1958, B. B. and Sue weren't traveling together so much, which posed its own problems. After a few years of this difficult routine, Sue King was no longer the girl of eighteen who had first met B. B., and as she grew up her ambitions had changed. After hoping in vain that her husband would be able to get back to Los Angeles more often, and would also involve her in the management of his career, Sue King asked for a divorce in 1966, at a time when B. B.'s fortunes were at their nadir.

Quite apart from the theft of his bus, which he had recently had to replace as a matter of urgency, King had just been stuck with a bill by the IRS, who were after a small matter of seventy-eight thousand dollars in back taxes, and there was now even less chance of his being able to come off the road and spend time with his wife. King was very upset by this second divorce, which he thought unfair. Once more a victim of the rejection he sang about every night, he even considered giving up music and going into business. If his tax debts hadn't forced him to carry on touring, he would probably have returned to broadcasting, meanwhile also managing the motel and service station which he was planning to build on land he owned in Tennessee.

In fact, it seems we have the U. S. Treasury to thank for the fact that B. B. King is still performing.

5
B. B. AT THE FILLMORE
(1966–1975)

B. B. King's second divorce in 1966 was a turning point in his life. His career had started in Memphis, but, with success, he had realized in the early fifties that it was too limited a setting for him. Houston was the home of his agency and of the ACA studios where he had recorded in 1953, and he lived there briefly, but Los Angeles soon became his base. Modern's pressing plant, offices and studios were there, in Culver City, and it was in the Los Angeles area that King had bought a house for his wife soon after they married in 1958. The aftermath of his divorce eight years later was drawn out and painful, for Sue King was claiming sizeable alimony payments, as well as the California house, all at a time when King wasn't in great financial shape.

Not long afterwards, he made the important decision to move to New York. There were personal motives: he wanted to put a physical distance between himself and his wife, feeling as he did that she had betrayed him by leaving. Equally, there were professional reasons: the Shaw Agency and ABC-Paramount, who handled his live appearances and his records respectively, were based in New York. More than Los Angeles, or any other American city, New York was home to advertising agencies, to the major TV and radio networks with their studios, and to publishers and others on the management side of the music business.

In strategic terms, this was a wise decision, since it allowed King to develop his contacts in the world of show business. Moving to the Big Apple was a vital turning point in his career. Within a few months he would break out of his musical ghetto and become a big name at the box office. It helped that fashions had changed, and were at last smiling on him, but that King was in a position to profit from the change was the doing of one Sidney A. Seidenberg.

Since leaving the Buffalo Booking Agency and moving to Shaw, King had had a succession of managers of varying ability, who had not concerned themselves with anything beyond the day-to-day. The most recent of them was a man named

Louis Zito, who had been King's manager for a few years by 1968, when a financial dispute arose between them, as King thought that Zito was ripping him off. B. B. and his manager then decided to call in Sid Seidenberg, a chartered accountant who worked for a large Manhattan firm specializing in show business. By a strange twist of fate, King and Seidenberg had already crossed each other's paths in 1944 when they were both stationed at Camp Shelby, but segregation had prevented them from meeting each other. In 1968, music and business finally brought them together.

After looking into matters for a few months, Seidenberg demonstrated his impartiality by reporting that Zito was in the right but also pointing out some shortcomings in the conduct of his management. Even though he had been shown to be in the wrong, B. B. King was impressed by the honesty and competence of the chartered accountant. "Shortly I noticed that a lot of the things that my other manager wasn't doin', Sid did them and wasn't my manager. That's how we became friends," King recalls.[1]

More than he needed a friend, B. B. needed a manager with initiative; after severing his links with Zito, he set about persuading Seidenberg to take charge of his affairs. "B. B. made me a manager," says Seidenberg with a smile. "I did not want to be a manager at first. I got involved in the music business straight from university as an accountant. I worked for many, many big artists and big managers as an accountant, so I understand the business from that end. I started with musicians and publishing. Like I worked with Tom Jones when he first came to the United States. I used to specialize in foreign acts coming to the United States, and black acts who felt that they had to find somebody they could trust. In the course of time, I represented Gladys Knight and the Pips for many years; I also represented Neil Diamond when he first started in the business.

"I used to do all the tax incorporations for all the musicians; that was my specialty and that's how I met B. B. He had a tax problem, and he was brought to me by his manager who was formerly a musician. When he came to me, it was a question of the use of funds, which is always the case. I reported the facts as they were to both parties. What am I gonna do? I mean I had to report to him, I wasn't gonna be bought off by anybody, and so B. B. saw that somebody was honest about it. I suggested that he get a new manager, and he did get another manager and that manager happened to have been a name person in Chicago. He was his very dear friend, that's why I'm not mentioning his name. He managed him and after three or four months [B. B.] came back into New York to meet me and he said, 'Sid, where is the money and the reports, and how are we doin'?' I said, 'You're doing lousy.'

He just said, 'Oh, my God,' went home and got on the telephone with this other guy. Then he came back to me and said, 'Please do me a favor and do it for a while.'

"I knew what a manager is and I don't like this business. I didn't like what they did to people, most of the managers. An accountant sees the inside of the business, and I was not crazy about what their ethics were. So I told him, 'Okay, B. B., only if you and I have an understanding.' He said, 'I'll do anything you tell me, as long as you think it's right, and if I ever think it's wrong I'll say it to you.' So we got started and it was taking up a lot of my time and I then agreed to become his manager."[2]

From the start, Seidenberg's objectives were in line with his new protégé's true abilities. No longer would it be a matter of settling for what the chitlin circuit had to offer, especially because the arrival of a racially conscious soul music seemed likely to make the blues no more than a historical curiosity. To win over an audience of white Americans and college students, B. B. King's name had to become familiar to all those people outside the African-American community who had never heard of him. "We reorganized his whole structure from that point on. We laid out a plan and the plan started to work, booking him in a different way, and changing agencies. What B. B. needed was exposure, even if it meant less money at first. He never had an organization, and I renegotiated all of his contracts, all of his copyrights. I'm publicity oriented also and I saw so many things that I felt should be done."[3]

Seidenberg was sure that carefully selected advertising endorsements would help make his new artist better known. In the late sixties, there were plenty of agencies on Madison Avenue looking to involve black Americans in TV commercials, in order to reach a sector largely forgotten by the small screen until then. B. B. King was a popular personality, well known in his community, and he had a positive image, especially among the housewives—one of advertising's main targets. So it was that in 1969 alone, King was involved in campaigns for Pepsi-Cola, AT&T and Axion soap powder. Quite apart from the money this brought in, from Sid Seidenberg's point of view these advertisements were achieving his initial objective, getting B. B. King's name and face known to the general public; since then, King has taken part in campaigns for Coca-Cola, Frito-Lay, Anheuser-Busch beer, and, more recently, Wendy's hamburgers and M&M's, all of which have increased his visibility.

Even more important was the cancellation of B. B.'s contract with the Shaw agency, which was only exploiting King's potential with the black R&B market, in Seidenberg's view. He felt that B. B. needed an agent who was familiar with African-American music, but was also convinced that modern blues could find a wider audience. There was no doubt that the man who best fitted the bill at that time was Joe Glaser, who had made Louis Armstrong an international star.

Accordingly, King joined Associated Booking, which Glaser had made the country's leading agency. Thanks to the company's contacts and reputation, work began to come from outside King's usual circuit; it was better paying, too, the more so because Glaser had immediately increased King's asking price to give him credibility with promoters.

These initial victories were not enough for King, however; he had realized that he would only be able to win over the wider audience long-term if his recording career took a new direction. In particular, it had to incorporate more daring production ideas. "Before I started working with B. B., he was basically an R&B artist, so the next move was to make him a big recording star," Seidenberg explains.[4] The aim now was not so much to sell singles to jukebox operators and the ghetto audience, but rather to issue polished blues albums that would be enjoyed by habitués of the big Las Vegas hotels and the fashionable New York nightclubs, as well as by jazz fans. It followed that ABC had to find new producers, who could give King's music an original tinge.

The changes that took place can be seen by considering the five LPs that appeared in the years 1967 to 1969. The first point to note is that the label they were issued on changed. Although he was still under contract to ABC, *Blues Is King* and its successors appeared on the subsidiary BluesWay label, which specialized in records aimed at comfortably-off Americans who could appreciate the vocal and instrumental subtleties of a musician like King, with his strong jazz influences. It was not by chance, either, that the sleeve notes were written by Sheldon Harris, an influential jazz critic and a mainstay of the magazine *Jazz & Pop*. Finally, changes among the producers used by ABC-BluesWay were also ample confirmation of the new direction King's career was taking.

For *Blues on Top of Blues* the company turned to bandleader Johnny Pate, who had already been used on several of King's earlier recordings, including the brilliant *Live at the Regal*. On this occasion, King distanced himself from the rough atmosphere of the clubs on the chitlin circuit, and used a set of tightly written arrangements, played with a sure touch by Johnny Pate's big band. Nevertheless, it was a smart idea of Pate's to have the king of the blues stick to a set of numbers that were appropriate to his image. Avoiding the trap posed by sentimental ballads, Pate contented himself with adding brass responses to the twelve numbers King had composed for the sessions, of which the splendid "Worried Dream" is a perfect example: it consists of an authentically bluesy subject ("When I woke up this morning, the tears was runnin' down my face / You know I guess I was dreamin', oh, that some other man was takin' my place"), and heartrending guitar phrases, punctuated by brief riffs on saxes, trombone and trumpet. Together, these elements build a dramatic structure, in which the tension is resolved by explosive brass figures.

In December 1967 King returned to the studio, this time working with Bob Thiele, a well-respected jazz producer who had already recorded T-Bone Walker for BluesWay. *Lucille*, the album that emerged from these sessions, was intended as a tribute to King's guitar and a showcase for his instrumental prowess. The title track was a chance for B. B. to hold a free-ranging conversation with his guitar, meanwhile recalling crucial episodes of their life together. "I'm very crazy about Lucille. Lucille took me from the plantation, or you might say, brought me fame," he confided, before praising his six-stringed companion by comparing her with some of America's biggest stars. It's significant that the artists B. B. named in this amazing ten-minute dialogue between voice and guitar were Frank Sinatra, Mahalia Jackson, Sammy Davis, Jr., and Ray Charles, rather than (say) Bobby Bland, Little Milton or Fontella Bass. King was obviously bypassing his usual audience and speaking to mainstream America.

Another important point about this third BluesWay album was that it saw a reunion between King and Maxwell Davis, whose arrangements had been so important to the Modern recordings of the previous decade. Alongside Davis was a veritable who's who of California R&B, including the likes of pianist Lloyd Glenn (formerly with Kid Ory, T-Bone Walker and Lowell Fulson) and tenor sax screamer Big Jay McNeely; together, they gave the band a wonderful jazzy sound. Percy Mayfield's standard, "I Need Your Love," is a perfect example of the album's well-rehearsed, yet seemingly effortless, atmosphere.

There was to be no new album as such in 1968, but it was this year that saw one of Sidney Seidenberg's biggest ambitions realized, when B. B. King was approached by Hollywood for the first time. Along with advertising and records, the movies were one of the main vehicles Seidenberg hoped to use to build up King's career. That was why ABC was the cornerstone of his plans: quite apart from its radio and TV networks, the company had important financial stakes in Hollywood.

Since finishing work on *Guess Who's Coming to Dinner* in 1967, Sidney Poitier had been looking for a production company to finance the filming of a screenplay he had written about a turbulent love affair between a truck driver and a maid. Eventually, Poitier came to an agreement with the film company owned by ABC, and shooting began on *For Love of Ivy*, starring Poitier and the singer Abbey Lincoln. The soundtrack was entrusted to Quincy Jones, a master of the genre, who produced a superb original score. There were some scenes where a radio was playing in the background, and Jones wanted to use new songs, rather than ones that were already around; he chose B. B. King to perform them. In all, three sides were cut in Hollywood during August 1968, and "You Put It on Me" and "The B. B. Jones" even managed to be fair sellers for King in the fall of that year. In addition to his own vocals, "The B. B. Jones" featured those of African-American poet Maya Angelou, who also wrote for B. B. "Get Myself Somebody," a song that appeared on a BluesWay 45 shortly afterwards.

ABC's policy seemed to be bearing fruit in the charts of both *Billboard* and *Cash Box*. More specifically, the album *Blues on Top of Blues* put King back into the Top Ten thanks to "Paying the Cost to Be the Boss," and "I'm Gonna Do What They Do to Me" spent a few weeks in the hit parade as well. However, the producer who found the winning formula for B. B. King was undoubtedly Bill Szymczyk, who worked on the next two albums.

Szymczyk—who later produced the Eagles with much success—had decided early in life that he wanted to work in music. He had started as a sound engineer, and gained a reputation in the business as an ace at the fast-growing science of mixing. Previously, the relatively primitive nature of recording had limited the producer's role to choosing an arranger and a set of songs. With the arrival of multiple-track recording studios, proficiency at mixing had gradually become an essential part of the producer's armory, and Bill Szymczyk, like Quincy Jones, was one of the experts.

To Szymczyk also goes the credit for the idea of putting a live side and a studio side together on one album. The result of this daring experiment was *Live & Well*. The "Live" section was recorded at a memorable concert at the Village Gate, an exclusive watering hole for New York's élite. Alongside the usual standards like "Don't Answer the Door" and "Sweet Little Angel," B. B. triggered shouts of approval from his new audience with "My Mood," an instrumental tour de force, and especially with "Just a Little Love," which he introduced with the words: "This is a brand new tune. A brand new tune! The band don't know it, you don't know it, and I don't know it either!" Actually, this "improvisation" was well prepared, being largely based on an old number cut for Modern in 1957, "Early Every Morning."

The result was an accurate record of a good concert, but Bill Szymczyk's genius was more apparent on the "Well" side, made at the Hit Factory, a fashionable New York studio. Szymczyk's aim was to sell B. B. King to a young audience by emphasizing his electric guitar playing, and providing a more rock-oriented backing than had been customary. To this end, Lucille was allowed free expressive rein, while rock-blues pianist Al Kooper and Gerry Jemmott, King Curtis's regular bass player, were called in to help. "There was something else I wanted to try," Szymczyk wrote in his liner notes to the album, "and the more we talked about it the more excited B. B. became. We got together, what I consider to be, some of the best young blues musicians in the country and locked ourselves in the 'Hit Factory' for two nights. The results of those two nights are the 'Well' side of this album. The music is all B. B. King but in a slightly different surrounding. There's an incredible amount of energy that's lacking in a lot of blues music today."[5]

For good measure, and to keep a touch of R&B in the recipe, Szymczyk had asked Johnny Pate to take care of the brass arrangements on some titles, like "I Want You So Bad." This track is a model of its kind, thanks to the perfect symbiosis between Gerry Jemmott's prominent syncopated bass playing and the riffing of the wind instruments, which are notable for their restraint and good taste. The customers who propelled four of the album's ten titles into the charts knew what they were doing. The biggest hit was "Why I Sing the Blues," a brilliant account of three hundred years of exploitation of black people in America, composed by King and Dave Clark, formerly a record plugger for Peacock and an occasional songwriter. B. B. was at his most convincing on this almost militant anthem to the blues, listing with poignant pride the stages in the painful rite of passage endured by African-Americans: "When I first got the blues, they brought me over on a ship / Men was standing over me, and a lot more with a whip / Everybody wanna know why I sing the blues / Well, I've been around a long time, I've really paid my dues."

Hoping to maintain the momentum, Szymczyk reunited the same musicians, and went back into the studio six months later, to try to recapture the special atmosphere of *Live & Well*. Considered as a whole, this second attempt, *Completely Well*, was disappointing, for it tended to overdo the very elements that had made *Live & Well* so appealing. On this second Szymczyk production, the vocals take second place to the guitar in a context of long, uninspired jam sessions. A notable exception, however, was "The Thrill Is Gone," the final track, which largely makes up for the album's defects.

"The Thrill Is Gone" was not an original number; King borrowed it from the California singer Roy Hawkins, whose "Why Do Everything Happen to Me" he had already recorded some years previously. As soon as one hears it, one recognizes that King's version of this tale of lost love is one of his finest performances, in the same class as his greatest blues numbers from the Modern days, such as "Sweet Sixteen" and "Blind Love." Over a layer of agonized heartbeats from Gerry Jemmott's bass, B. B. and Lucille engage in an insistent, despairing dialogue, which allows little room for the slightest optimism. Bill Szymczyk brought all his production and mixing skills to bear on this track, especially with his very tasteful use of violins and cellos, which endow the whole performance with a remarkable seriousness.

"My producer . . . was just starting on the scene, and his ideas reminded me of the old Bihari days. He wouldn't interfere with you while you were recording. . . . Don't misunderstand me. I know this was a different time, and some of us need coaching. I'm one, but only to a point. . . . Allow me to express me as I am. Let me play as I do. Don't say, 'Sound like this person,' or, 'Do you remember hearing the record so-and-so?' Well, that kind of attitude makes me not want to be on record because I like to be myself.

"Bill Szymczyk was a young producer and he understood me, one of those types that bring out the best in you. . . . That's the way it was the night we recorded 'The Thrill Is Gone,' one late night. . . . I told Bill, 'I've got this tune I've been carrying around for about eight years. Every time I record I've never been able to do exactly what I want with it, and this rhythm section is cookin'! I think that I want to try this!' He said, 'Fine, go ahead.' And we went into 'The Thrill Is Gone' and man, it was just like hand-in-glove. It clicked for me, but not for him. So we finished about two-thirty in the morning. I said, 'All right, we're gonna knock off.' . . . About two hours later, I get a call and he's all excited, . . . 'What do you think about adding some strings? . . . Man, that's a good pop record.'

"So he got a guy called Bert DeCoteaux to do the strings. About three or four days later I went down to hear the strings being put on and they did give it a different flavor from what began on record. I liked it and when 'The Thrill Is Gone' was released, my crossover began."[6]

Entering the *Billboard* best-seller lists on 3 January 1970, "The Thrill Is Gone" closed the book on a decade that had often been difficult for B. B. King. Over the next three months, the song reached number three in the soul charts, but above all it made number fifteen in the U. S. Top 100, and became the first of King's songs to make an impact on America as a whole—eventually earning B. B. his first Grammy Award. As such, the commercial success of "The Thrill Is Gone" was proof that a major change had occurred in the nature of B. B. King's audience. After several years of trial and error, he had finally managed to "cross over," and win over white America, thanks to Sid Seidenberg.

Despite Seidenberg's earlier expectations, the change wasn't spearheaded by middle-class jazz fans. The psychedelic artwork on *Completely Well* and the use of rock-oriented backing musicians were clear signs that B. B. King's new audience was to be found on university campuses, not in Las Vegas casinos. The first producer to realize this was Bill Szymczyk, who had put his faith in the young Greenwich Village audience ever since recording *Live & Well*'s concert segment.

Ten years earlier, King was still being scorned by New York intellectuals, who rejected his electric blues because of what they saw as its vulgar commercialism. Until 1968, B. B. King was ignored by college students, who preferred the quaint "country blues" of musicians like Son House and Mississippi John Hurt; he had hardly ever appeared before young white audiences—maybe with the exception of college fraternities at the beginning of his career in Memphis—and when he had, the results had been uniformly disastrous.

Since the mid-sixties, however, some of the fans who had discovered the blues through acoustic performers at folk festivals and in campus coffee shops had gradually developed an interest in more modern blues styles. To begin with, Muddy Waters, Sonny Boy Williamson, James Cotton, Little Walter and Howlin' Wolf had turned student audiences on to electric blues; later, white disciples like Mike Bloomfield, Johnny Winter and Elvin Bishop in the United States, and Eric Clapton and John Mayall in Great Britain, would make a point of telling startled audiences that, where electric guitar playing was concerned, their mentor was one B. B. King. That name meant nothing to the great majority of white blues fans, for all that it identified the blues' chief spokesman in the black community. As the seventies began, it was the success of "The Thrill Is Gone" that was to resolve this paradox.

There had been a number of harbingers of change before "The Thrill Is Gone" hit big. At the end of 1967, after twenty years in the business, B. B. had appeared for the first time in a white New York club, the Cafe A Go Go in Greenwich Village. In his eyes, though, the real turning point came a few months later; in the summer of 1968 he was booked to appear at the Fillmore West, a venue in the black area of San Francisco which had become one of the temples of hippiedom.

"The last time we had played there it was 95 per cent black, in 1963," he declared to a *Newsweek* reporter during the spring of 1969, while taking a break from making a singing commercial for soap in a New York studio. "This time it was 95 per cent white. I was shocked. Mike Bloomfield introduced me as the greatest bluesman. I didn't know if I should walk out there. When I finally did, they gave me a standing ovation. I wanted to cry. Words can't say how I felt."[7]

B. B. King's new audience were the people who went to hippie promoter Bill Graham's Fillmore West, and later attended huge rock festivals like Woodstock. King's favored status with them was largely due to Lucille, his guitar. The rock music that was celebrated at Woodstock was symbolized by the electric guitar; it was the badge of a new and explosive culture, whose most radical exponents, like

Jimi Hendrix and Pete Townsend, participated in the cult of the electric guitar by burning or methodically smashing their instruments on stage. King, as the main creator of urban blues—the style that was the basis of rock music—suddenly found himself at the center of developments, hence his remarkable success.

In just a few months, rock music and its stars enabled B. B. King to become much more widely known. "Until the days of rock 'n' roll, a lot of the places just wouldn't accept us. In some of these places, the door's open now for you to go into. . . . Mike Bloomfield, Elvis Presley, the Beatles, Fats Domino, and people like that helped us out quite a bit."[8] In February 1969 he appeared in Memphis's conservative Peabody Hotel at a convention for the entertainment organizers of the major American universities, who quickly made him one of the biggest attractions at campus concerts. In August, he performed in Atlantic City, where he and Little Richard were hailed as founding fathers at a festival featuring pop acts like Iron Butterfly, Creedence Clearwater Revival and Janis Joplin.

There was no question, as far as King was concerned, of betraying his roots and abandoning the chitlin circuit audience, and he continued to appear regularly at the Burning Spear in South Side Chicago, the Prince Hall in Detroit, and the Club Handy in Memphis. Even so, such appearances at the big ghetto clubs became rarer even as better-paying offers flowed in to his booking agency.

The new opportunities that were opening up were of three kinds: rock audiences, jazz fans, and the international market that was beginning to develop for urban blues. On the rock side, King was welcomed to major venues like the Fillmores (East in New York, West in San Francisco), the Tea Party in Boston, and the Ash Grove—a Los Angeles folk club that also featured electric acts—as well as to the festivals that were a feature of the period. A good example of the latter was the Festival Mar y Sol, which took place in Puerto Rico in spring 1972, cheerfully mixing John McLaughlin's mystical jazz, Dr. John's gumbo-rock, the rock-blues of the Allman Brothers, and Herbie Mann's Latino jazz-rock, all in a cloud of pot smoke.

Another important episode in B. B. King's burgeoning career on the rock music scene was his participation in a 1970 tour by the Rolling Stones. Mick Jagger and his colleagues wanted to pay their respects to the blues by presenting the sources of their inspiration to their concert audiences. The same year, Buddy Guy and Junior Wells had opened the show on their European tour. In the United States, it was B. B. King's turn to present the blues to a rock audience at eighteen sold-out concerts. "My audience had started mixing before that, but that really pushed it over the top. A lot of people heard me on that Rolling Stones tour that hadn't heard of me before. I remember once in Baltimore, one white lady came out, she had teenagers who seemed to be impressed with what I did. She came up to me and asked, 'Have you made any records?' "9

On the jazz side, B. B. King's music had received the seal of approval from fans who were taking more and more notice of the gospel and blues that lay at the roots of the music. One of B. B. King's first major appearances in this context happened in 1967 at the Monterey Jazz Festival, where he shared the stage with one of his all-time heroes, the Texan guitarist T-Bone Walker. At that time, a concert like this was unusual for a blues singer, and the fact that it was televised made it all the more conspicuous. In 1969 the Ann Arbor and Newport festivals welcomed King and his band.

In May 1970, B. B. and Lucille were accorded the signal honor of appearing at the mythic Carnegie Hall in New York, at a concert billed as "B. B. King and His Friends." The friends in question weren't lightweights: among other stars brought together by producer Bob Thiele were the drummer Elvin Jones, saxophonist Eddie "Cleanhead" Vinson, and, above all, two great artists whose influence King had always proclaimed, Big Joe Turner and T-Bone Walker.

The New Orleans Jazz and Heritage Festival had been taking place annually since 1970, and from 1972 onwards King became a regular feature at this forum for African-American traditions. The 1973 festival stood out from the rest, though, because he performed with his cousin Bukka White for the first time since the legendary Beale Street days. The meeting of cousin Bukka's slashing steel guitar and Lucille's singing tones was a strange one, all the more so because the two men were accompanied at this one-off concert by the pianists Roosevelt Sykes and Professor Longhair and the rhythm section of New Orleans R&B group the Meters.

Finally, there were the tours that would henceforth take B. B. King and his band to the four corners of the world. Events like the American Folk Blues Festival had been bringing the blues to Europe since the early sixties, but King had to wait until early 1968 for his first appearances in the Old World. On 10 January, he played his first concert overseas in Strasbourg, France; five days later he appeared at the Salle Pleyel in Paris, where French critic Jacques Demêtre was waiting for him. Demêtre proudly recounted their meeting in the British magazine *Blues Unlimited*: "Backstage, where the Parisians Memphis Slim, Mickey Baker, Hal Singer and Dionne Warwick had come to meet their friend, I had the chance to see him again, nine years after our meeting in Chicago. He looked at me and suddenly laughed: 'You're from 'Jazz-Hot' . . . your name is . . . let me remember a little . . . Demêtre!' "10

After playing fifteen concerts across Europe, King and his band returned to the United States. In passing, it's worth noting that British promoters had so little faith in the drawing power of this unknown blues singer that on this first tour no bookings were to be had in Britain. As a matter of fact, bringing over an artist such as King seems to have been a major gamble for the tour organizer, who reduced the cost of the band as far as he could, even deciding that there was no need for a bass player! Things were very different a year later, when King returned with his full band, this time making his first stop in London. "We came through customs and there were about 2,300 people waving American flags. And as we walked through customs, everybody started hollering, 'B. B.! B. B.!' By God, I was frightened. . . . I'd never seen anything like that before. Never ever! I was actually like a superstar to them, at least, that's the way they treated me."[11]

In February 1971, it was Japan's turn to welcome him, in a very real sense, as an ambassador of the blues; no blues singer had ever played there before. Since then, King and his musicians have made innumerable tours in Europe, Asia and Australia. B. B. King has also been welcomed in Africa several times, making emotional journeys to the roots of his music. His first tour there was set up by the American State Department in December 1973, and took him to Ghana, Nigeria and Senegal.

British journalist and photographer Val Wilmer was in Lagos to report on the occasion, and her memories show clearly how B. B. saw cultural encounters like this as a mission. She writes, "Lagos was not quite ready for the Mississippi blues and B. B. was advertised as a 'Soul' musician, sharing the bill with Nigeria's King of Afro-Beat, Fela Anikulapo-Kuti. At a reception held at the United States Ambassador's residence, Fela, ever the rebel, shocked the diplomatic corps by using bad language and attacking American imperialism. B. B. made a better impression, painstakingly answering questions from journalists who knew more about the Beatles than the blues. . . . [W]hether on television or in concert, [he] made a point of presenting his music in a historical and sociological context. 'Maybe our forefathers couldn't keep their language together when they were taken away, but this—the blues—was a language we invented to let people know we had something to say,' he told an audience at Lagos University. 'And we've been saying it pretty strongly ever since.' "[12]

Another important pilgrimage for B. B. was his trip to the Holy Land a few years later. For someone like Riley King, who had grown up hearing the Promised Land talked about every Sunday at his mother's Baptist church in Kilmichael, playing in Israel was a bit like bringing down the walls of Jericho. Appropriately, perhaps, King himself came tumbling down shortly after he arrived. "Yes, I fell about nine feet and messed up the side of my face and my shoulder, and busted a blood vessel in my left hand. My teeth went right through my lip—seven more stitches. But I went swimming that evening in the Dead Sea. I couldn't miss it, man, because we were sold out in Jerusalem. The Holy City—I *had* to make that!"[13]

His overseas tours also made B. B. more famous in the United States, of course. In less than three years, King had become a celebrity who was as likely to be found at Las Vegas or Lake Tahoe as on the major talk shows that had ignored him for so long. "Let's put it like this, I been doing what I'm doing for twenty years and I haven't made but one major TV show and that was Steve Allen's," he had once complained shortly after appearing on this show in 1968.[14] Given the importance of the visual image, it comes as no surprise that Seidenberg had factored TV into his plan. Accordingly, King made several prime time appearances on the major networks, climaxing in 1969 with Johnny Carson's *Tonight Show*. The following year, he sang a medley of his greatest hits on the *Ed Sullivan Show*. For the record, Carson would invite King to appear twenty-seven times on his show, including the last one in May 1992.

After the Beatles mentioned B. B. King in a song on their *Let It Be* album, it even became fashionable for New York society to turn up at his concerts. When Jackie Onassis came to a show at Manhattan's Bottom Line, the gossip columns were full of the news, and Sid Seidenberg was delighted with the resulting publicity. The great names of show business didn't want to be left out of the picture, and George Benson, Lou Rawls and Johnny Winter were among those who followed in Ray Charles's footsteps by making friends with King and playing short jam sessions with him on stage.

The presence of famous guest artists was also a feature of King's ABC albums through the seventies. *Indianola Mississippi Seeds*, produced by Bill Szymczyk in 1970, was the outcome of an encounter between King, the rock pianist Leon Russell, and Tin Pan Alley singer-songwriter Carole King. In sound and spirit, this album was the logical follow-up to "The Thrill Is Gone"; there were plenty of Szymczyk's trademark violins, and Lucille was as important as King's singing. The results found favor with purchasers, who made three of the record's nine titles into hits, among them "Chains and Things," which made the Soul Top Ten, and "Ask Me No Questions," which appeared in the Pop Top Forty.

B. B. King in London and *L.A. Midnight* depended even more heavily on famous names to attract the pop audience. The former, recorded in London as its name indicates, brought the cream of British rockers into the studio with him. Drummer Ringo Starr, guitarists Alexis Korner and Peter Green, pianist Pete Wingfield, and a swarm of carefully respectful acolytes took turns to surround B. B. King with musical affection, but, despite their best efforts, in the end his voice and guitar were drowned out by a confusing mixture of styles and sounds. Apart perhaps from "Ghetto Woman," which charted in 1971, nothing on this record has endured.

L.A. Midnight was a better-focused musical encounter. Half the album was instrumental, and although rock-blues made its presence felt through contributions from Taj Mahal and his guitarist Jesse Ed Davis, the emphasis was on King's rhythm and blues roots, with the use of legendary California session musicians like Plas Johnson, Red Holloway, Red Callender and Earl Palmer.

The harking back to R&B was even more obvious on the next LPs, which saw a decided return to ballads. This was especially true of *Guess Who*, the title track of which—a pop-blues that King had already borrowed from the black crooner Jesse Belvin ten years before—set the tone. By 1972, pop music had changed, and 1969's sounds were old hat. ABC and Sid Seidenberg therefore decided to concentrate on the slightly older audience that King had acquired from his regular concert seasons, held in the main urban centers and aimed at the middle classes. Seidenberg's new policy was confirmed by the considerable success of King's first appearance at Caesar's Palace in Las Vegas with Frank Sinatra's blessing, and further confirmed by a contract for several years with the Las Vegas Hilton.

Between 1973 and 1977, the next four albums—*To Know You Is to Love You*, *Friends*, *Lucille Talks Back* and *King Size*—maintained the sentimental mood; the first of them did better than the others, with "I Like to Live the Love" and Stevie Wonder's fine composition "To Know You" entering the Top Forty of the *Billboard* pop charts. Nevertheless, by concentrating excessively on ballads, King lost a good deal of his musical essence, as purists were not slow to point out. It has to be said that, in artistic terms, with rare exceptions blues lovers found less and less to enjoy on King's albums. The fact was, to make a point in his and Sid Seidenberg's defense, that these albums were much more rewarding financially than the early recordings had been; more creative though those undoubtedly were, their sales had been confined to the R&B market.

However, blues fans had a chance to rediscover the old-style B. B. King in great form on two albums shared with his longtime friend Bobby Bland. Since 1973, when Don Robey had retired and sold Duke-Peacock to ABC, Bland and King had both been on the same label. In 1974, it was decided to record these two giants of postwar Memphis blues jamming in front of an invited audience of friends and fans, among them James Brown, who made the trip specially to be present for *Together for the First Time . . . Live*.

In a very informal atmosphere, King and Bland spent two hours swapping memories of the days when the latter was the former's valet, meanwhile trying to outdo each other in humor and vocal inventiveness on a selection of their greatest hits. "Ladies and gentlemen, nothing is planned tonight. We didn't plan anything," King announced at the outset, just before Bland interrupted to offer him a beer. After a series of blues-deficient albums, this one was as refreshing for blues fans as the beer was for B. B., so much so that the LP became a best-seller and incited ABC to repeat the experiment successfully two years later on *Together Again . . . Live*, recorded at the Coconut Grove in Los Angeles.

In King's eyes, these albums were not a return to roots, for, unlike his critics, he didn't consider that he had ever abandoned the blues he had started out with. However, he admitted that he had made some changes; if he was accused of treason, he responded by speaking in terms of adaptation, while conceding that there had been compromises. "I think the blues have changed quite a bit. Something like life in itself in a way. In fact to me blues is life, because it's the past, the present, and believe it or not, quite a bit of the future. Basically I should say I'm still doing the same thing. I still feel 'Three O'Clock Blues' when I sing. I still feel 'Sweet Sixteen' or 'Sweet Little Angel' or any of the tunes I made in the late '40s, early '50s. But in order to get them on the radio today, I have to broaden them to whatever fad of music is being played at that time. I try to be smart enough to take my blues with the same basic feeling, but maybe change the beat just a little. If soul is big, I try to put a little bit of soul beat on it. If rock is on, you know, you put just a little bit of rock on it. But the basic blues are still there. And I don't think anything stays the same except change."[15]

B. B. King was the better able to put up with these criticisms because he had always done his best to get the blues recognized and accepted. Subsequently, he has often said that in America, to be a blues singer is to be black twice, with all the drawbacks implicit in such a position. So it was that in 1968 he decided to go back into the record business by founding the Virgo label, twelve years after his first attempt with Blues Boys Kingdom. This time, King's interest was centered on Larry Davis, whom he had taken under his wing when they met in Arkansas ten years previously. A superb singer and guitarist, Davis had had a moment of fame in the late fifties on Don Robey's Duke label.

In 1968, B. B. and Bobby King, his longtime road manager, had decided to give Larry Davis's career a boost by producing a single. Nevertheless, B. B. dropped the project fairly quickly, feeling that Davis's musical goals were too far from the blues: "Larry, I think, is a fantastic singer. I think he's a great artist . . . Bobby [King] wanted to do something mod like. I wanted to stay with another type of thing that I thought should have been done. But I had to agree with Bobby that the music was changing and times was changing. No need to fight progress. So, what he decided to do was to take Larry to St. Louis and Oliver Sain to produce it. So when he decided to do that, I said, 'Well, I'll tell you what, if that's the case then I'm gonna get out of it and you got it.'"16

It's hard to understand the way B. B. King's career has gone without taking account of his fundamentally activist nature. This activism sometimes spills over from promoting the blues, and is put at the service of other causes. In addition to his financial contributions to the NAACP and to Dr. King's movement, one of the most striking examples of this side of his character is his involvement in an organization devoted to the rehabilitation of prisoners, an idea that was born after he played at Chicago's Cook County Jail.

Recordings captured live in a jail or prison were coming into vogue around this time, and not only in the blues field, as Johnny Cash's recorded performance at Folsom Prison indicated. For his last collaboration with King, Bill Szymczyk thus recorded the concert that B. B. gave on 10 September 1970 for the inmates of the Cook County Jail, a notoriously tough penitentiary. Originally, King had been approached by the institution's new director, Winston Moore, an African-American who felt that B. B.'s blues were precisely what the inmates needed.

Like *Live at the Regal*, *Live at Cook County Jail* was an important episode in King's recording career. The pent-up emotions released by 2,117 mostly African-American prisoners, some awaiting trial and some convicted, are a counterpart to the spontaneous reactions of the middle-class audience at the Regal Theater. The prisoners saw King's visit as an all-too-rare recognition of their humanity. The playlist was a succession of slow blues during which B. B. and his audience established a rapport. "How Blue Can You Get," "Worry, Worry," "Three O'Clock Blues" and "Sweet Sixteen" were all evocations of separation and loneliness which held obvious significance for listeners subject to incarceration and isolation; King completed his show by holding out a hand to them with a very moving "Please Accept My Love."

The presence of the king of the blues in the depths of a prison was entirely appropriate; as B. B. observes, the prisoners in Cook County Jail had every reason to have the blues: "When I told the management that I was going to go into Cook County Jail in Chicago to do a benefit there, they said, if you're going there, let's do it right. Let's carry the press and take some recording equipment and record it. When we got out there we found that about 70% or 75% of the people in there were Black or of the other minority races, and very young, in their teens or early twenties. The press interviewed a lot of these people and found out that some of them had been there like a year almost and *still* hadn't even come to trial. They were just there, arrested, and they stayed there, couldn't afford bail. So the press really blew it up, man; they really worked with it that next day. I felt that was good, so the people on the outside could know what was happening behind the wall.

"I told them that from then on I would be glad to donate my services anytime they wanted them. I felt that the more I went in and played and the press went with me, the more we could let the people out there know. I feel that a lot of the judges and the people who arrest those fellows and put them in there don't even know what it *looks* like. I felt that if we kept it up long enough, some of these people would probably be invited to go in to see for themselves, and that might make them think a little bit different. Don't get me wrong, I don't think that when a guy does something wrong he shouldn't be punished, but if he *does* it as a human being, he should *pay* for it as a human being."[17]

Over the years, King's concern has never waned, and he has given free performances in correctional centers on some fifty occasions. In March 1972, as the craze for "live in prison" concerts tended to fade, King refused to give it up; he took his concern a step further when he and the well-known New York lawyer F. Lee Bailey set up the Foundation for the Advancement of Inmate Rehabilitation and Recreation. King comments on FAIRR: "I played Walpole prison out from Boston once, and I saw several of my friends who had been out of sight for quite a few years because they had been *in* there. Two or three of them told me that it wouldn't be so bad to spend ten or fifteen years some place if they knew that they would have something to depend on when they got out. . . . They told me, B. B., if we could get guitars, if we could get books, if we could just get something we could work with—and this hurt me so bad, thinking about a guy having to stay in a place for ten or fifteen years, and *nothing*, you know. I would probably be in prison today if it hadn't been for some folks caring about what I was doing."[18]

The blues had proved to be an unrivalled means of communication with American prisoners. In France, Australia and Japan, the blues could overcome racial, linguistic and cultural barriers. Its expression of personal experience awoke a real echo in the collective unconscious of his audiences: "When I sing a blues the whole song may not be about the person, but there are certain things in it that they will recognise that have happened to them, or some of their friends, and when this happens, they feel it."[19] In ten years, B. B. King had won over a worldwide audience without cutting himself off from his origins. Once begun, this trend continued and flourished in the years that followed.

6
THE PLAN FULFILLED
(1975-1997)

A good deal has been written about the relative importance of the manager and the artist in nurturing a career. Some say that talent is the sole motor of success, while others believe that business management is more important than artistic ability. No doubt the truth lies somewhere in between. All the same, the greatest successes in the world of show business have been achieved by famous teams, like Satchmo and Joe Glaser, Elvis and Colonel Parker, Dylan and Albert Grossman. In B. B. King's case, there are other factors reinforcing the theory that his success is due to a skillful mix of innate talent and imaginative management.

The way King's career took off as soon as Sid Seidenberg replaced Louis Zito in 1968 was the first indicator of this. Nor can it be coincidence that the sudden crisis B. B. suffered through in the latter half of the seventies was triggered by his deciding to part company with his manager.

By 1975, King and Seidenberg had known each other for seven years, and each had come to appreciate and value the other. King admired his manager's instinctive business acumen, while Seidenberg had a deep respect for B. B.'s acute intelligence, his sensitivity and his creativity. To outside observers, there was nothing to indicate that trouble was brewing, or that their relationship was about to be affected by the seven-year itch.

The source of the disagreement was partly petty professional jealousy. Once King had induced him, almost by chance, to go in for artist management, Seidenberg had given up his accountancy business to launch S.A.S. Incorporated, a firm which specialized in representing artists, and which took its name from his initials. Along with managing B. B. King's career, Seidenberg was also overseeing that of another important name in African-American music, the singer Gladys Knight and her group, the Pips.

Since the late sixties, Knight had seldom been absent from the upper reaches of both the soul and the pop hit parades. In 1973, she even achieved her first double number one, taking "Midnight Train to Georgia" to the top of the *Billboard* pop and soul charts. With her subsequent records repeating the process, Seidenberg had decided to concentrate heavily on Knight's flourishing career. At the same time, although King had no doubt acquired the fame he deserved, it must be said that he was a long way from achieving the level of commercial success with his records that was enjoyed by Gladys Knight and the Pips. This is hardly surprising, of course, given that King was twenty years older than Knight, and that his music didn't have the same pulling power with the youngsters who bought her sophisticated soul singles.

Nevertheless, King saw the time and effort which Seidenberg was putting into fostering Gladys Knight's career as a betrayal. When Seidenberg managed to negotiate an important television contract for Gladys Knight and the Pips in July 1975, King felt that he was being unfairly neglected, and decided unilaterally to leave S. A. S. Rather than looking for a new manager, he decided that he could run his own affairs, and began by breaking a rule that Seidenberg had thought it advisable to make when they had decided to team up. "The first thing I did when I took over in 1968 was to get rid of the bus," Seidenberg recounted to Charles Sawyer. "The first thing he did when he went out on his own in 1975 was to buy another bus. Right away it broke down; he had to get a new engine."[1]

Early in 1978, King and Seidenberg began making overtures to one another, with the half-acknowledged intention of getting back together. Things were not going as well as either of them would have liked. B. B. didn't have the business contacts that Seidenberg had used to get his career moving. He had relocated from New York to Las Vegas in 1975, which further cut him off from the expertise of the record industry, and made his gambling habit even more hazardous. In three years, none of the albums he had cut for ABC had achieved real success, for want of an imaginative producer who could breathe new ideas into them. *Together Again . . . Live*, his second album of duets with Bobby Bland, was the best of them, even if the formula wasn't as fresh the second time around. *Lucille Talks Back*, produced by B. B. himself, and *King Size* were too gimmicky to appeal to blues fans, and not innovative enough to attract the wider audience, with the result that King's name had almost vanished from the American charts. On the other hand, his concert diary was not quite as full, and B. B. knew that sooner or later the fall in sales of his albums would affect his touring work.

As for Sid Seidenberg, he had suffered a long series of setbacks with Gladys Knight and the Pips. Since 1975, Gladys had married and become a mother, which created tensions among the members of her group, who were unhappy with the way their careers were slowing down. In 1977, she and the Pips split up, and Knight decided, with encouragement from her ambitious husband, to go her own way and dispense with the services of S. A. S. Deprived of his star attraction, Seidenberg suddenly needed B. B. King if his business was to survive at all, and the two men were officially reconciled in 1978, with each admitting their respective wrongs.

From this second honeymoon onwards, Seidenberg resolved to direct his protégé's affairs energetically. To celebrate their reunion, he began with a masterstroke, organizing a tour of the U. S. S. R. for King. Setting up a series of concerts in a closed country like the Soviet Union was a considerable achievement, requiring several months of delicate negotiation and the resolution of numerous bureaucratic hassles imposed by the Soviet authorities. For instance, the cultural attachés at the Soviet embassy in Washington asked to attend a concert by the B. B. King Orchestra, and even required a complete transcription of the songs King planned to sing before giving their agreement.

The end result was worth all the difficulties Seidenberg had encountered, and the twenty-two-concert tour which took place in 1979 was a triumph. B. B. retains an emotional memory of the welcome he received, from Moscow to the steppes of Central Asia, and from Leningrad to Tbilisi: "We just came back from the Soviet Union. We was over there for a month, for the State Department on a cultural exchange program over there. I'd like to tell you that the Soviet Union will never be the same. We left 'em a lot of blues, over there; I think they already had a few!" he proudly told his audience back home.[2] "Some years ago, it was in '79 to be exact, I was in the Soviet Union, they called me the father of jazz. I liked that very much because I feel that the blues was here before jazz, and I feel that what we've contributed to jazz, the roots are still here. Kind of like father and son, beans and rice."[3]

This tour had considerable repercussions for King in the United States, for in the eyes of his fellow citizens it gave him an image as an ambassador for American culture as a whole, rather than simply for the blues. At the same time, overseas engagements came thick and fast, and anyone who saw King then will remember his exceptional concerts. As a result of his international success, King had once again been able to enlarge his band, and was now heading a line-up of a dozen musicians for the first time since the height of his success in the early fifties.

Not only that, but his bandleader, Calvin Owens, was a veteran of those days who brought great authority to his direction of the five-man wind section. Phil Blackman on piano was an intelligent musician who gave King's repertoire a solid gospel sound; finally, the rhythm section, consisting of Leonard "Wine" Gill on guitar, Russell Jackson on bass and veteran drummer Calep Emphrey, Jr., gave the ensemble a strong Chicago blues feel. Unlike the bands he had worked with during the first twenty years of his career, the 1979 orchestra was at least one-third white, a further sign that King's blues were aimed firmly at the wider audience.

One of the constant features of King's recorded work has been the regular appearance of live LPs. The live double album made at the University of Mississippi in 1980 is typical of this happy period of his career. "We got some old ones for you tonight, and we got some new ones for you tonight,"[4] King told the audience before launching into a wild version of Louis Jordan's theme song "Caldonia," which kicked off his show. Faithful renditions of his greatest hits followed, as well as three new titles from the album *Midnight Believer*, which had put him back on track after his reunion with Sid Seidenberg.

The main sign of Seidenberg's return to the helm, even more than the overseas tours or the concerts in Las Vegas, was the recording of albums which had none of the relative weakness of King's previous product. Seidenberg's number-one aim was to get back the dynamism that had been blunted over the years and to find a producer with the ability of Bill Szymczyk. In 1978, indeed, he made use of a whole team of producers, bringing together Stewart Levine and the jazz group the Crusaders. Nesbert "Stix" Hooper, Wilton Felder and Joe Sample had started out in Houston as the Swingsters, named after the style of jazz they played. Changing their names to the Jazz Crusaders, then to the Crusaders, they had made a name for themselves since the early seventies as a first-class cocktail lounge act.

Guided by Stewart Levine, and playing numbers composed by Joe Sample and Will Jennings, King and the Crusaders collaborated on two LPs, *Midnight Believer* and *Take It Home*. "Stewart is really a professional producer. Stewart is an old friend of mine, and I brought him into the picture originally. He used to produce the Crusaders, and he had concept ideas," Seidenberg says. "And B. B. never had a concept album like that before."[5]

There was a lot riding on these experiments, and Seidenberg persuaded ABC-Dunhill to launch *Midnight Believer* with a big party at the fashionable New York nightclub Studio 54. It was a highly profitable investment, because for the first time in ten years King's sales figures were comparable to those he had achieved thanks to Bill Szymczyk; his new repertoire seemed to be winning over the wider audience without offending the sensibilities of the purists. The Crusaders' music, while staying faithful to the jazz tradition, was bright and swinging enough to appeal to everyone.

King's "Crusaders period" lasted until 1981, when Joe Sample and his colleagues invited him to join them on an international tour. Their London concert was especially meaningful for B. B., because he appeared with a symphony orchestra for the first time. For Riley King, the orphan boy from Mississippi whose education hadn't gone past elementary school, appearing on stage at the Royal Festival Hall backed by the Royal Philharmonic Orchestra was a triumph over the circumstances of his upbringing and the climax of all his striving.

In late 1981, still under the guidance of Stewart Levine, King returned to R&B, his first love, making *There Must Be a Better World Somewhere* for MCA, which had bought ABC in 1979. A pair of blues medics, Doc Pomus and Dr. John, were called in alongside B. B. to provide the songs for this album, and the veteran saxophonists Hank Crawford and Fathead Newman, both formerly members of Ray Charles's touring band, supplied the all-important touch of swing. "I remember one of the songs we were fooling with at that time we titled 'There Must Be a Better World Somewhere,' " Dr. John recounted in his autobiography. "Later B. B. King picked up this song and used it as the title song for his *There Must Be a Better World Somewhere* album. The song came out of this old hymn I knew from New Orleans called 'This Earth Ain't No Place I'm Proud to Call Home.' . . . There was something very special about that tune. B. B. won a Grammy for it. . . . Before the record came out, B. B. sent Doc a picture of the album cover and Doc, who usually threw stuff like that away, hung it on the wall."[6]

The following year, B. B. was back in the studio with Stewart Levine. With Ray Charles's success twenty years earlier in mind, Levine intended to present B. B. King in a country and western setting. "This is the greatest album I have recorded in my thirty-five years in the music business. It represents my lifetime dream in expressing my feelings through music and song and puts together all my roots and influences from blues to country and everywhere else. It is something different but yet the same," King wrote in the liner notes.[7]

Recorded, needless to say, in Nashville, *Love Me Tender* was a complete disaster commercially. Neither MCA nor the critics liked the idea, much to the displeasure of Sid Seidenberg, who had had great hopes for it. "It's a beautifully produced album, actually it's B. B.'s best-produced album. It's not that it's bad stuff, but it didn't get the right exposure, it didn't get the right record company support, and it didn't get the right direction. Some of that stuff is fantastic stuff that will eventually see the light of day, I believe."[8] The listener who can forget that King is a blues singer is bound to admit that *Love Me Tender* succeeds completely. Charley Pride had already shown that African-Americans can sing C&W as well as anybody, and King confirms it brilliantly. His velvet voice blends miraculously with a set of songs borrowed from such giants of country music as Willie Nelson and Conway Twitty and writers Mickey Newbury and James Holiday, and the brass arrangements played by the Muscle Shoals Horns are perfect. But it has to be said that, although this record is a superb specimen of country-soul, B. B. King's usual audience was bound to react to such a venture with baffled disapproval.

The resounding failure of this album put a temporary stop to the collaboration between B. B. King and Stewart Levine. On 16 September 1982, his fifty-seventh birthday, King cut a transitional album whose title, *Blues 'n' Jazz*, was a clear signal of its purpose; for Sidney Seidenberg, who took on the producer's job himself, it was intended to reassure King's audience after the debacle of *Love Me Tender*, and it obviously succeeded since it earned its author a Grammy.

From 1985 onwards, B. B. resumed his forward march with a new producer, David Crawford, and in particular with a project which involved film director John Landis. "I brought David back into the business. He was the brilliant producer who had done the ABC album *To Know You Is to Love You* [in 1973]," Seidenberg recalls. "David was out of business; I found him down in Florida. He wasn't doing too well—financially very bad shape—and he was working with a guy named Luther Dixon who was an old writer that I knew many, many years ago. For that *Six Silver Strings* [album], David was really broke and I gave him another shot. He wrote two or three of the songs, he wrote a couple with Luther. I knew Henry [Stone] so I said, 'We're gonna be in Florida, and we're doing a couple of gigs in the area, so why don't we use your studio?' He was starting over again at that time. He let us have it any time we wanted, it wasn't busy, it was one of those kinds of things. And that's why we recorded in Henry Stone's studio. Then in '87 or '88, I got a phone call that David had overdosed and that was the end of Mr. Crawford,"[9] Seidenberg remembers with a touch of emotion.

In addition to Crawford's work, *Six Silver Strings* included three songs from the film *Into the Night*. Even more than any of his albums, B. B. King's presence at the heart of the musical segments of this John Landis film was a major media coup which gave his fame a considerable boost. Landis had been a fan of King's for a long time, having discovered him when his friends Dan Ackroyd and John Belushi were regularly inviting the king of the blues onto their TV show *Saturday Night Live*. The soundtrack of *Into the Night* had been entrusted to the composer Ira Newborn, to whom Landis gave very specific instructions: "I presented Ira Newborn with this problem; compose a motion picture score to feature a particular player and not compromise his unique talents or the integrity of the movie."[10]

With his characteristic lack of confidence, King initially asked himself if he could properly carry out the job entrusted to him, but finally realized that film music was well within his capabilities. "I was really excited about it, but then I started to think, 'Why me?' When there's, oh, Leonard Bernstein and many more people. . . . We went and had a meeting. In fact [Landis] wanted to hear some of it. And then he went on to answer my questions, you know, why me. He went on to say, 'Well, you've influenced a lot of people, and I'm a fan, and I know a lot of other people are, so I just would like to use you.' And, man, my feet didn't touch the ground for quite some time. I really stayed in the air, you know, over that. And I started to think, though, because I was leaving shortly for Europe, and I started to think as I've thought many times growing up, every time something that I really wanted to do, like if I wanted to play baseball on the Fourth of July, it would rain.

" . . . I was never really relieved until it was released, because I had kept thinking that they may stop the project anytime, or they may not like what I was doing, or just something, . . . and then when you know anything, it's gone to somebody else.

" . . . I was really tensed, all the time, and after they had finished the movie, . . . they set me down in a room, big studio, alone, and they put an amplifier in there with me, you know, and just let me play to the scenes as they roll 'em off and I thought somewhat like the piano players. They used to play behind silent movies. . . . And finally when it was released, then, it was the first time that the tension had ever really left."[11]

Besides appearing as himself in the movie, B. B. King sang three numbers on the soundtrack, which were given heavy airplay as video clips on MTV. This marked his return to favor with a younger audience for whom this was the only way to get acquainted with his music. Still working with the composer Ira Newborn, King was back in the film studios in 1986, this time to sing a song for the Martin Scorsese film *The Color of Money*. Evidently B. B. King spelled box office to Hollywood, and he was in demand again in 1987 for the soundtrack of Mike Figgis's *Stormy Monday* and for a small part in *Amazon Women on the Moon*. During the following years, he would also make a number of cameo guest appearances on television programs, including *Baywatch*, *General Hospital*, and the Cosby show.

There were other signs, too, that blues was no longer on the blacklist as it had been twenty years earlier. In 1984, during a concert at the Beverley Theater in Los Angeles, King was unexpectedly joined on stage by Michael Jackson and Prince, who wanted to show their respect for King and his music. The trend was further confirmed in 1987 when King was honored with a Lifetime Achievement Award by the National Academy of Recording Arts and Sciences; this prestigious award, established in 1962, is reserved for performers "who, during their lifetimes, have made creative contributions of outstanding artistic significance to the field of recordings." This was clearly the case with B. B., whose cohonorees that year were a prestigious and eclectic group: Fats Domino, Roy Acuff, Enrico Caruso, Billie Holiday and Igor Stravinsky. On October 18 of the same year, he was also one of the fifteen new inductees into the Rock and Roll Hall of Fame.

"One of the things that helped," King explains, "the contemporary players like the late Stevie Ray Vaughan, Robert Cray, Jeff Healey, what I call the new kids on the block, that's been a big help. A lot of the people that know them, a lot of 'em didn't know us. They are now learning about us through these people. Back in the sixties, through my association with the Rolling Stones, it was a bit different. A lot of the rock stars was playing blues music, but they wasn't blues musicians. In other words, they were rock musicians playing blues! Of course it helped, it opened a lot of doors for us. I'm very happy they did, but it's very few of them that decided to actually become blues musicians, at that time. Now why I mentioned Robert Cray and Stevie Ray [Vaughan], it's because they're known as blues musicians, and they are superstars like the rock stars were at that time."[12]

In 1988, it was the turn of the Irish rock group U2 to pay homage to the master of the electric guitar by offering him "When Love Comes to Town," the standout title on their album *Rattle and Hum*; tactfully, they arranged for him to record it at the Sun Studio in Memphis where he had cut his first sides for RPM. Thanks to the airplay it got on MTV, "When Love Comes to Town" has played a crossover role somewhat similar to that of "The Thrill Is Gone" twenty years earlier. But unlike Fats Domino or Ray Charles, whose success with mainstream America was achieved thanks to pop-oriented material, King owes a large share of his worldwide popularity to his flirtation with the rock players, thus confirming the strong link between electric blues and hard-core rock. "My association with U2 made a big difference," King states. "We were playing in Dublin, Ireland. We were there and they came out as a guest one night. They came backstage after the concert, we chatted backstage, and when they were about ready to leave, I asked Bono if he would write a song for me, and he said he would, and it started from there. So he did, and the song later became a hit, I toured with them in '89 and part of '90, and that tour did a lot for B. B. King. A lot of the young people that listen and like rock 'n' roll, they've been introduced to myself through U2, including through video and television."[13]

It seemed as though young people couldn't get enough of B. B. King, and the American establishment was not to be left behind. At the invitation of the late Lee Atwater, former chairman of the Republican Party and George Bush's campaign manager during the 1988 elections, B. B. visited the Oval Office in the spring of 1989, and even gave a much-admired concert at the Kennedy Center for the Performing Arts in January 1990 to honor the president on the first anniversary of his inauguration. Since then, according to Sid Seidenberg, there haven't been enough days in the year to take up all the concert offers he receives. The period 1990–91 was an especially busy time, with three B. B. King CDs issued. "We did two live albums. We did *Live at San Quentin* first, then we did the one at the Apollo with the Philip Morris Orchestra. We even won a Grammy for *Live at San Quentin*—which surprised even me," says Seidenberg.[14]

Live at San Quentin shows that B. B. has stayed faithful to his work on behalf of prisoners, but unfortunately lacks the force of *Live at Cook County Jail*. All through King's concert, one senses a violence and a latent aggression among the inmates of San Quentin, which makes the album's tense atmosphere even more oppressive.

Live at the Apollo is very different. In the fall of 1990, King gave his musicians a holiday, and took the chance to make an international tour with the big band sponsored by the tobacco giant Philip Morris. King visited Taiwan, the Philippines, South Korea, Japan, Australia, Turkey, Germany, the Netherlands, France and Italy, finishing this twenty-concert series with a show at the mecca of African-American music, Harlem's Apollo Theater. Everybody who was anybody in New York was at this concert, which was recorded at Seidenberg's request.

Apart from the fact that he was sharing star billing with his old friend Ray Charles, it was the prospect of working with a big band that justified the decision for King. "My manager asked if I would like to tour with the Super Band. My answer was yes, since I love to travel and I love to go places and I like to meet people and I like good music, and these guys are playing good music and I enjoy it. You know, Count Basie's band with Jimmy Rushing, to me, was one of the great old-time togetherness, if you will. If I could fit in with this orchestra as well as Jimmy Rushing fitted in with Basie I'd be a very happy guy.

"There are people that listen to [the Philip Morris Orchestra] that are not aware of B. B. King per se. So when these people come out to hear the super orchestra, they get a chance to hear B. B. King. So I get the benefit of that."[15]

This was not the first time King had worked with a big band. His 1956 orchestra and the one of the early eighties had been almost similar in line-up to the Philip Morris Band. However, not even Maxwell Davis's brilliant arrangements in the great days at Modern had given him the feeling of power that he got from playing with veteran jazz musicians like the saxophonist Plas Johnson, the guitarist Kenny Burrell, the bass player Ray Brown and trumpeter Harry "Sweets" Edison—to name just a few of the members of the Philip Morris Orchestra—with their many years' experience in big bands.

The Philip Morris tour gave King the chance to realize a very old dream of his, which he had already spoken of in the sixties, during an interview with the sociologist Charles Keil: "I've been studying arranging, reading Schillinger, because what I would really like is a band that echoes my guitar—like Ray [Charles]'s band sets off his piano playing. I've had guys do arrangements for me that weren't bad; and my musicians are OK, but they play standard things behind me. I won't really feel like an artist—you know, gone as far as I can go—until I get me some arrangements that really add a third part to my guitar and voice and make everything fit together just right."[16]

In the fall of 1990, the dream became a reality. After B. B.'s success on this first tour, the Philip Morris foundation asked him to do another series of concerts the next year. Directed by pianist Gene Harris, this new version of the Philip Morris Super Band numbered seventeen musicians. Between Brussels on 21 October 1991 and Pittsburgh on 24 November, they played nineteen concerts in ten countries, among them Hungary, which marked King's debut in Central Europe.

During a stopover in Paris, King and Seidenberg took the chance to promote King's latest album in France. *There Is Always One More Time* had just appeared in the record racks. The issue of a new disc is always an exciting moment for an artist and his entourage. It was all the more so with *There Is Always One More Time*, because to B. B. and his manager it seemed like the climax of the plan that Seidenberg had put into operation in 1968. "MCA, we're an American company owned by a Japanese conglomerate, distributed by BMG, a German company," Seidenberg says. "And they're [MCA] a great company, they have a new president who is a fantastic guy, he is a man of his word. We have a great deal now, B. B. King gets amply rewarded for his efforts finally after twenty-five years. We have not reached the rock star level, but we have reached the popularity and visibility around the entire world for B. B. King. We're much more than one step higher.

"The company did more in four weeks than they did in the last twenty years," Seidenberg adds. "See, this record is now being released worldwide. It's out around the whole world at one time, and it's popping out in different parts of the world. I mean it's a home run with this record, and we gotta make this record not just a blues hit, a pop hit, a jazz hit, but every kind of hit in the United States first."[17]

There Is Always One More Time was very successful on the artistic level. First, it marked King's reunion with the Crusaders. As well as featuring their work, the disc also includes two excellent tracks written by the young African-American guitarist Arthur Adams and a tribute to Doc Pomus, who had recently died. The great simplicity of these titles is especially remarkable: no choirs, no brass, just a rhythm section made up of American session superstars like the drummer Jim Keltner and keyboard player Neal Larsen. The project was supervised by Stewart Levine, definitely one of the key players in Sid Seidenberg's master plan. "Stewart produces Simply Red, too, you know, not just the Crusaders," says Seidenberg. "Now he produces a lot of other people, very successfully. I have an affinity with Stewart and his feeling, and he's followed the same pattern. He's able to extract talent from people, and he has a nice way to deal with B. B. For the new album, he got Will Jennings, who was the number-one writer in the United States. We recorded the album live with B. B. at every session, which is unusual.

"Stewart Levine started his section and B. B. had two weeks off, so he went to California and he replayed every track. It was so wonderful, he was having such a terrific reaction to it, and his playing was fantastic, his singing was superb, I mean it was different. And then Doc Pomus was dying, and he had submitted four, five songs, and 'There Is Always One More Time' just happened to hit everybody at that time, so we did that song as a love song. We rushed the track to him after it was finished; flew from L.A. to New York twice, and then the next day he died after he heard the song, so we titled the album *There Is Always One More Time* because it fit perfectly with the situation," Seidenberg concludes.[18]

Over the years, just like anyone else, B. B. has seen friends and relatives come and go. For someone to whom love is as important as it is to him, the death of someone close is inevitably felt as a betrayal of life. His baby brother, his mother and his grandmother, a teenage sweetheart, a black man who was lynched before his eyes when he was living with his father in Lexington . . . too many people have died around him, all before he was a man. More recently, in the early eighties, Albert Lee King died, and B. B. had to accept the fact that his father would no longer call him "Jack." The death of Doc Pomus, just before the release of *There Is Always One More Time*, was also painful. "He's a friend, a true friend of mine. We kept in touch, but sort of like some family members who don't write or call every week. But once or twice a year I had a chance to see him and always talked with him, and he was that kind of person. He like brought sunshine to people. That's the kind of person."[19]

Despite its good qualities, however, it was not *There Is Always One More Time* but the next release which brought B. B. King's talent to worldwide notice. Issued in spring 1993, *Blues Summit* appeared at the ideal time to benefit from the blues' sudden return to fashion in the early nineties. All over the world, it became the thing for music stars to incorporate some blues into their repertoire, and even to invite the best blues musicians to share in their glory for a moment. Thanks to the privileged place he occupies in the history of the music, B. B. was one of the first to ride this new wave, duetting with Gary Moore, Ray Charles and Grover Washington, Jr., to name but a few.

The *Blues Summit* concept—suggested by Andy McKaie, who is in charge of MCA's blues catalog—was inspired by this development. Track by track, King was joined by some of the greatest names in rhythm and blues, from Lowell Fulson to Ruth Brown, by way of Joe Louis Walker, Buddy Guy, Koko Taylor, Irma Thomas, Etta James. The strength of the disc didn't arise solely from the amazing list of artists; alongside this who's who of blues were the cream of the session musicians, including the Memphis Horns, trumpeter Ben Cauley, guitarist Mabon "Teenie" Hodges and saxophonist Lee Allen. Above all, though, the choice of songs displayed the rich diversity of African-American popular music: Chicago blues with Junior Wells's "Little by Little," rock 'n' roll with Leiber and Stoller's "You're the Boss," R&B with "We're Gonna Make It," first recorded by Little Milton in 1965, a beautiful reading of Ivory Joe Hunter's "Since I Met You Baby," and even the musical gumbo of New Orleans, represented by Chris Kenner's "I Like It Like That."

Radio program planners were quick to appreciate this splendid CD, which could be heard on every radio station in the United States all through 1993, while King was undertaking a triumphal "Blues Summit" tour all across the country. To keep up the momentum, MCA put out a compilation entitled *Lucille and Friends*, featuring the most important collaborations from his career.

The formula seems to have appealed to B. B. and Sid Seidenberg, for the next CD, *Heart to Heart*, also preserved a musical meeting: this time the maestro and Lucille met up with vocalist Diane "Deedles" Schuur at the Capitol studio in Los Angeles. A technically exceptional singer, this blind artist specializes in ballads and love songs, giving them a humorous, salty delivery that is reminiscent of Dinah Washington. B. B.'s usual fans were a little disoriented by finding him in this sentimental, jazzy context, but the experiment did bring King to the attention of the audience for singers like Tony Bennett and Frank Sinatra, something Seidenberg had always wanted to do.

To date there have been no new releases since this 1994 production, apart from occasional guest appearances, like the live recording made in Austin in May 1995 for a *Tribute to Stevie Ray Vaughan* CD on which he sang a gritty version of the late Texas guitarist's "Telephone Song." There has been talk for some time of a solo record, no doubt to cash in on the "unplugged" fashion given its impetus by Eric

Clapton, but nothing substantive has happened on this front. This long silence is all the more surprising in that B. B. King's name has never been more prominent. In 1994, a notable year, there was a series of sold-out concerts in South America and a Far East tour that took B. B. to China, where he helped inaugurate the Hard Rock Cafe in Beijing. Two years later, he received the Kennedy Center Honors from the hands of President Bill Clinton, while the publication in the fall of his autobiography, written in collaboration with the journalist David Ritz, was another proud moment. But undoubtedly the highlight of 1996 was seeing his name at the top of the bill for the Southern Jamboree which closed the Atlanta Olympic Games on 4 August.

The year before, B. B. celebrated his seventieth birthday. He did so fairly quietly, perhaps because at that stage of one's life the start of a new decade is not something to be taken lightly. People close to him have been dying with increasing frequency of late, among them his most famous namesake, Albert King. During his forty-year career, B. B. King has seen a good many of his colleagues reach the end of the road, sometimes abruptly. When discussing the problems created by the insecure life of a traveling musician, King regularly recalls the tragic deaths of Johnny Ace in 1954 and Sam Cooke, killed in 1964 at the height of his popularity and in very suspicious circumstances. He does this not so much to ward off fate as to remind himself yet again that his success is a fragile construction, which the slightest false step could do away with for good. Talent is not enough; it has to be managed. You need determination, patience and obstinacy to get to the top of the heap.

Or to use Sid Seidenberg's favorite expression, you need a good plan. "B. B. is now as well known as Mick Jagger or Bob Dylan. B. B. is in the movies in America, we've had a syndicated radio show throughout the eighties, we're on popular television in America, we're doing children's programs, we're doing lectures at universities as a leading authority on blues, and we get paid the same as celebrity people who go on lecture tours at universities. So we've reached a lot of levels on a lot of different markets with B. B. See, B. B. is an industry with like twenty different divisions. Rather than me have twenty acts, I have one act with twenty divisions—seven people who work all of the time on B. B.'s career. Twenty-five years it took us to get here! But it was part of our plan from the start."[20]

7
LUCILLE

B. B. King's music revolutionized the blues in the postwar years, but paradoxically it has acted as a brake on change since then. Many observers have formed this opinion, even if few have expressed it. One writer who hasn't shrunk from frankness is Gérard Herzhaft in his *Encyclopedia of the Blues*: "[H]is success made him incredibly influential with other musicians: almost all the guitarists who performed after 1950 are indebted to him, when they don't copy him exactly. Even in Chicago, where the influence of the Delta blues was dominant until the end of the fifties, the success of Otis Rush and Buddy Guy around 1958, who were original guitarists but openly acknowledged his influence, demonstrates the domination of B. B. King's style.

"This domination is overwhelming: today, nine blues guitarists out of ten play like B. B. King, not to mention the scores of singers who imitate him."[1]

For African-Americans, B. B. King's name has long been synonymous with electric blues, as is shown by the pseudo-B. B.'s who have been in evidence in ghetto clubs since the sixties, like Andrew "B. B." Odom and Alvin "B. B. Jones" Nichols. The longest-serving of these imitators was undoubtedly Albert King, whose real name was Albert Nelson, and who claimed that he was B. B.'s brother for years, before establishing himself as an original artist with a style very much his own.

Interviewed by sociologist Charles Keil in 1965, B. B. King himself reflected on these "wanna-B's" with philosophical amusement: "Man, there are at least four little B. B.'s or B. B. King juniors running around now—one in New York, one in Chicago, one in California, I even heard of one back in Mississippi. If the name helps them get started, I don't suppose I mind much. I just hope they grow out of it. But it makes me feel good to be copied, makes me think the fourteen years I've spent in this business haven't been in vain. Being an influence makes me happy, and keeps me on my toes too. I always have to stay a little ahead of them."[2]

In more recent years the tradition has continued, with Artie "Blues Boy" White, "Blues Boy" Willie, Gary "B. B." Coleman and even a B. B. Queen! The case of B. B. Coleman is an interesting example. In the world of the blues, nicknames can come about in various ways: sometimes a musician adopts a sobriquet himself, hoping to boost his image by acknowledging a more famous artist's influence; sometimes, as in the late Gary Coleman's case, it's the audience that awards such a badge of honor to a favored musician. Coleman's style owed as much to Albert as to B. B. King, but he was christened "B. B." by his admirers simply because he was a blues singer who played guitar. The nickname "B. B." has become shorthand when the African-American audience wants to designate someone as a talented guitarist, and B. B. King has come to mean "blues guitarist" in the same way that "Hoover" means vacuum cleaner.

In the rock music world, King undoubtedly inspired the development of the electric guitar in the progressive rock era, whose chief exponents, including Eric Clapton, Michael Bloomfield, Jeff Beck, Jimmy Page and Johnny Winter, were all influenced by him. "At first I played exactly like Chuck Berry," Clapton says. "Then I got into older bluesmen. Because he was so readily available I dug Big Bill Broonzy; then I heard a lot of cats I had never heard of before: Robert Johnson and Skip James and Blind Boy Fuller. . . . I was about seventeen or eighteen. When I came back up in it, turned on to B. B. King and it's been that way ever since. I don't think there is a better blues guitarist in the world than B. B. King."[3]

King has been a tremendous influence on modern urban blues because his is a tremendous talent. It would be wrong to hold it against him personally, but one cannot help noting that the originality of his musical ideas has stifled the impulse to develop further in many of his followers. The blues world is full of musicians, of varying originality, whose music starts with King, among them Buddy Guy, Buster Benton, Larry Davis, Little Joe Blue, Eddy Clearwater, Mighty Joe Young, Eddie Kirkland, Luther Allison, Robert Cray, Eddie C. Campbell, Lurrie Bell and Otis Rush; even Son Seals has occasionally borrowed from B. B.'s repertoire, and there are many others whose names could be added to the list.

The lyrical single-string style that King developed has become so commonplace in modern blues that it would be quicker to list those who have not fallen under its spell. The outstanding names here are Fenton Robinson, who is heavily influenced by jazz, Hubert Sumlin, and Earl Hooker, the great slide player who died prematurely, and who was a master musician before B. B. King had made his first record.

King's disciples come from all over the United States, and work in different regional styles, but on reading their names, one is struck by the preponderance of Chicago blues artists, the immediate heirs of the Delta tradition. This is all the more significant in that it was B. B. King who broke out of the enclosed musical world that had been the lot of Delta musicians. Probably because it held such a dominant position in the Windy City, the Delta blues was largely resistant to outside influences for a long time. By opening himself to other idioms and new sounds, B. B. King turned things around, and drew on styles that had hitherto taken some of their inspiration from Mississippi blues. It is probably because of his achievement in blazing new trails and enabling a renewed creativity that the Chicago musicians offer him their unparalleled respect, and eagerly imitate him.

It's clear that King has been heavily influenced by the music of Mississippi, which he heard from his earliest years. His recordings teem with numbers from the mid-southern tradition, like "Eyesight to the Blind" and "When My Heart Beats Like a Hammer"—tributes to the two Sonny Boy Williamsons—or "Shake It Up and Go" and "Rock Me Baby." A recent example comes from a concert at San Quentin Prison in California; after playing "Never Make a Move Too Soon," then a late seventies number written by Joe Sample of the Crusaders, he made a striking step backwards with one of the oldest Delta themes, "Catfish Blues."

Nevertheless, King's chief inspiration, strangely enough, comes from the blues of Texas and Oklahoma, and, to a lesser degree, from New Orleans. It's hard to figure out exactly why King was attracted to styles that came from outside his immediate musical environment, but there were probably two factors. First, his mother's family was deeply religious, and the blues was very marginal at home. Until quite late in life, King had little contact with Delta blues musicians. The major exception was his cousin Bukka White, but he was doing two years in Parchman Penitentiary when King began to play the guitar. "My people were very religious and I was afraid to sing the blues around the house. My aunt . . . would get angry with anyone singing the blues, I would have to do that away from the house," he remembered later.[4]

B. B. King learned in church, especially as far as singing was concerned. Before his first experiments with Reverend Archie Fair's guitar, Riley had performed many times for the Kilmichael congregation since his mother had first encouraged him to do so as a four-year-old boy. There was little or no blues on the radio, but there was gospel music, and King was especially fond of programs by the Fairfield Four, a quartet from Nashville, Tennessee. To this day, one of his idols is Sam McCrary, the Fairfield Four's lead singer, whose elaborate melodic lines and dramatic delivery can be heard in King's singing style. Gospel also taught King how to vary the dynamics within a number, by contrasting extreme tension and release.

Here, too, King was unusual in Mississippi, where it's more common for a blues singer to turn to gospel music when the fires of youth have burned out than the other way around. King is well aware of the strangeness of the change that he underwent, explaining it in terms of his army hitch, which broadened his musical horizons rather than reinforcing his religious convictions: "It was when I went into the army that I started singing blues. A lot of fellows seemed to get religious and sing spirituals when they got in there, but me, I didn't."[5]

It wasn't just philosophical or spiritual considerations that prompted this change; material factors had a part to play, too. "While sitting on the street corners playing, people ask me to play a gospel song. And when I'd play it, they'd always pat me on the shoulder or something and compliment me very highly: 'Son, you're good. If you keep it up, you're gonna be all right one day.' But they never tip. But dudes who would ask me to play a *blues* song would always tip, man, give me a beer."[6]

The second factor accounting for Riley King's eclecticism is his personal taste. B. B. says that, rather than listening to records by the Delta greats, he always preferred the 78s of other artists he heard at his great-aunt Jemimah Stells's house when he was five or six years old, even though he had no idea where these musicians came from: "My aunt used to buy records like kids do today, and some of her collection was Blind Lemon [Jefferson], Lonnie Johnson. She had Robert Johnson, Bumble Bee Slim, and Charlie Patton. . . . But my favorites turned out to be Blind Lemon Jefferson and Lonnie Johnson. . . . I've got some of [Blind Lemon's] now—I keep them on cassette with me. . . . His touch is different from anybody on the guitar—still is. I've practiced, I tried, I did everything, and still I could never come out with the sound as he did. . . . He was way before his time in my opinion."[7]

Blind Lemon Jefferson, a singer-guitarist from Texas, was one of the founding fathers of the blues, along with Blind Blake on the East Coast and Mississippian Charlie Patton. Jefferson's style is characterized by the alternation of chords, arpeggios, and single-string runs, and there are influences from outside the culture of rural black Texas, such as the rhythms and melodies of Hispanic-Americans of Mexican descent. Lonnie Johnson, born in New Orleans in 1899, was a major source of inspiration for the great creative musicians in both blues and jazz. He freed the guitar from being just an accompanying instrument, and is rightly considered the initiator of its role as a soloing instrument. Between them, Johnson's sophisticated playing and Jefferson's diverse sources of inspiration were the basis of the West Coast blues that flourished after America entered the Second World War.

The very jazzy California blues, and the southwestern blues from which it sprang, were the roots of B. B. King's inspiration, and he made judicious use of them to lend color to his music. Nearly all his favorite guitarists from the forties onwards came from this musical school. Among them were Johnny Moore, who was Texas singer and pianist Charles Brown's regular accompanist and the source of King's liking for ninth chords; Moore's brother Oscar, whose velvet chords and nimble solos featured prominently on Nat "King" Cole's first recordings; Bill Jennings, of Louis Jordan's band; Lloyd "Tiny" Grimes, whose sense of economy counterbalanced Art Tatum's astoundingly profluent piano playing; and Charlie Christian, a pioneer of the electric guitar, whose work B. B. first encountered in a bar, on a soundie of the Benny Goodman Orchestra. "Charlie Christian was amazing," King remembers fondly. "I first heard him around 1941 or 42. There were 10¢ vending machines then like juke boxes, but with pictures. You put in a dime or quarter and you could see the most popular people of the day. That's how I first saw Duke Ellington, Louis Armstrong, Count Basie, and Louis Jordan. And that's how I saw Charlie Christian."[8] It was Christian's use of exotic chords in his solos that especially impressed King. "During the time of Charlie Christian, most people weren't aware of chords like ninths and thirteenths. So, what Charlie Christian was really known for was using those progressions. He used what we call diminished chords, and, man, he could break them up so pretty. He just lay 'em out—breaking up those diminished chords—and still had a good rhythmic pattern going along with it. Well, that to me started the improvising. . . . The guitar doing those diminished chords made it stand out just a little bit different from what some horn players had been doing."[9]

Undoubtedly one of the biggest impacts on King, though, was his discovery in the mid-forties of T-Bone Walker, the undisputed pioneer of the electric blues guitar. Going into town one Saturday night after a week's work on the plantation, he heard electric guitar blues for the first time when he found Walker's famous "Stormy Monday Blues" on a jukebox. The narration of his first encounter with the man in person, a few years later, gives some idea of the esteem in which he has always held Walker, his inspiration as far as the electric guitar is concerned: "I was working as a disc jockey at station WDIA in Memphis, Tennessee. I was the same as I am today. I'd come in about ten minutes before I was to go on the air, and that's late! So when I arrived, I heard this piano in the next studio from me, and one of the announcers came over and said, 'Do you know who that gentleman is at the piano there?' I said, 'No,' because he had his back to me and I'm trying to pull out my records. . . . 'It's T-Bone Walker, that's who,' the announcer ended up. Wow! I drop the records right there! I take another look to see this fellow is sharp. T-Bone was a dresser, too. And it was T-Bone all right—my idol, next door. I went in and he greeted me real nice, and I'm saying to myself, 'I'm shaking hands with the man who made me get the electric guitar!' "[10]

Texas and the West Coast didn't just influence King's instrumental approach—far from it. At first his singing, initially gospel influenced, matured as he listened to the big names of prewar blues, like the pianist Leroy Carr, the remarkable singer Peetie Wheatstraw (nicknamed "the Devil's son-in-law"), and the enigmatic Doctor Clayton, whose brilliant compositions, like "The Woman I Love" and "I Gotta Find My Baby," were a prominent part of King's recorded repertoire from the first. "Dr. Clayton was the man that I used to idolize," King remembered in 1965. "Just about everything he did, I used to sing along with it for hours."[11] Nor should we forget the big names of early country music, who were widely broadcast, and who influenced several generations of blues singers, B. B. King among them. If this seems an unlikely line of descent, it should be remembered that King's great-aunt had records by Jimmie Rodgers in her collection, that Gene Autry was often featured in the movies B. B. saw as a teenager, and that the first song he played on guitar from a fifty-cent instruction book ordered from Sears Roebuck, "Oh My Darling Clementine," wasn't exactly a blues standard. "I listened to Gene Autry, and I listened to Jimmie Rodgers and Roy Acuff. Most of the country stars I was around then, I was able to hear them on the radio later. My boss had [recordings of] country players like Hank Snow, and I could go on and name quite a few that was popular at that time. . . . When I was trying to learn to play guitar—I would get these country tunes in these guitar books [and] I was learning country even when I didn't intend to. These books had mostly country songs, like 'My Darlin' Clementine,' 'You're My Sunshine,' 'Walking the Floor Over You.' . . . So I learned to read them before I could play 'Three O'Clock Blues.' "[12]

As a mature artist, though, King would distance himself from his first mentors, and draw inspiration from the best-known Texan vocalists, like those who sang with the swing bands that were popular from the thirties onwards. Rather than the lowdown, yearning songs of the traditional blues singers, King favored the humorous, danceable numbers of blues shouters like Wynonie Harris, Joe Turner, Jimmy Rushing and Roy Brown, who sang over a dense backdrop of piano boogie and roaring saxophones. "I heard Charlie Christian and this is when I began to get kind of acquainted with jazz. This is when he was with Benny Goodman. And at the same time, I used to listen to Jimmy Rushing and he was with Count Basie. So you see the link? By listening to them, I began to get interested in big bands."[13]

He borrowed a lot from these vocalists—numbers like Wynonie Harris's "Baby Look at You" and Joe Turner's "Sweet Sixteen"—but another essential source was undoubtedly Lowell Fulson. Originally from Oklahoma, Fulson became one of the founders of the California blues sound after settling in the San Francisco Bay area on his return from war service in the Pacific. It will be recalled that "Three O'Clock Blues," King's first hit in 1951, came from Fulson; a few months later, King drew on another of his compositions, "Midnight Showers of Rain," for "Some Day Somewhere," hoping to capitalize on the formula that had been so successful. As for "Every Day I Have the Blues," the composition popularized by Memphis Slim that was a best-seller for King in 1955, his version is clearly indebted to the one Fulson had made with pianist Lloyd Glenn a few years earlier. Finally, in 1960 "Blue Shadows" confirmed King's affection for Fulson's music.

Generally, it's noticeable that B. B. King has been very successful with his West Coast repertoire. As well as the compositions mentioned above, he has recorded a series of wonderful Percy Mayfield numbers, including "Strange Things," "Please Send Me Someone to Love," "I Need Your Love" and "Half Awake," which he recorded as "You're Still a Square." Above all, though, there is "The Thrill Is Gone," which has become a centerpiece of King's live appearances wherever he plays. "Believe me, if I didn't sing 'The Thrill Is Gone,' they'd throw rocks at me," he jokes.[14]

This song had first been a hit in 1951 for its composer, Roy Hawkins. Little is known about Hawkins, except that he lived in Oakland in the late forties, and that his talents brought him to the attention of Modern Records at about the time that B. B. joined the company. Hawkins had two hits for Modern, first with "Why Do Everything Happen to Me," which he wrote in a hospital while recovering from a car accident, then with "The Thrill Is Gone." King obviously admired Hawkins's music, for he recorded the former title in the late fifties, ten years before his famously successful version of the latter.

Another major West Coast artist who was important to King's development was Ivory Joe Hunter. This Texas pianist and singer had settled in California in 1942, and it is to him that King owes his immoderate affection for the tender ballads and sentimental numbers that have always been a vital part of his repertoire, both live and on disc. "I Almost Lost My Mind," "Since I Met You Baby" and "Bad Luck Blues" are among the compositions by Hunter that King has performed over the years. There's a fitting symbolism in the fact that it was "Blues at Sunrise," one of Hunter's greatest hits, that got King his job at WDIA, when he sang it at his 1948 audition for the station manager. Ever since, ballads have been part of King's singing style, and another defining difference between him and the Delta's other great originals. "You Know I Love You," "I'm King," "I Love You So," "Please Accept My

Love" and "Guess Who" are among the hits he has had in this vein, of which his African-American audience is very fond.

Finally, it is impossible to talk about King's musical roots without mentioning Louis Jordan, a seminal figure in rhythm and blues, whom B. B. admires unreservedly, along with his guitarist, Bill Jennings. Jordan was a singer and saxophonist, born in Arkansas, whose career was atypical; rather than going into blues like so many of his contemporaries, he decided to make a career playing in bands of all kinds but mainly in jazz ensembles. After working in outfits led by Clarence Williams and Chick Webb, Jordan founded the Tympany Five in the late thirties, playing an exuberant, funny brand of music which drew on jazz, blues and pop.

Apart from borrowing numerous items from Jordan's repertoire—among them the celebrated "How Blue Can You Get"—King has also inherited his mantle as a master of the shuffle, a development of the eight-to-the-bar boogie-woogie rhythm which the Tympany Five brought to a peak. For an artist like King, accomplished at varying the dynamics of a show, the shuffle allows him to avoid the danger of monotony inherent in a succession of slow blues, and at the same time gives him a chance to show off his instrumental and vocal dexterity. As he explained in the early seventies, "A lot of my early work was influenced by Jordan. Even today it still is. I have tapes here of his recordings and I'm just about to do another of his tunes, which I've renovated. His was called 'Jordan for President,' and mine's gonna be 'B. B. for President,' which is his original idea. Jordan should have made it bigger than he did. Later, when Bill Haley came along, Decca had him and they had no need to revive Jordan, who was doing what Haley did long, long before Haley."[15]

If this seems like a remarkably varied set of sources of inspiration, it should be pointed out that, since his childhood days spent listening to his great-aunt Jemimah's records, King has remained at heart a fan and a collector. By the time he donated his collection to the University of Mississippi in the early eighties, he had amassed thousands of records, acquired over many years and in many places. Even today, one of his main pastimes, in the rare moments of peace when he is at home in Las Vegas, is putting performances by his favorite musicians on cassette, so that he can listen to them on the road.

When he is touring, his bags overflow with these tapes, which he takes everywhere, including into his dressing room. He sometimes shares his enthusiasm with a visitor, like André Fonteyne, who interviewed him at the July 1989 Rhythm & Blues Festival in Peer, Belgium. "I'll show you something right now. I have Sonny Boy Williamson, the first Sonny Boy Williamson. In fact, if you go to my hotel room now, you find Blind Lemon [Jefferson], you find Lonnie Johnson on cassette.

I have a lot of Lonnie Johnson, all of them in fact, just to show you, I didn't know I was gonna see you, right? So I couldn't try to be kinda impressive to you. Now these people I mentioned are all here, Blind Lemon, Lonnie Johnson. . . .

" . . . But I'm not complaining. I do buy records, I buy a lot of records—and a funny thing about it: I'm so happy today to buy records that I listened to then, you understand? Records that was available in '49, '50, '51. Now when I'm playing them, oh my God! I'm so happy to get them. . . . Things that I used to hear and you can't hear anymore, oh I find them and I treasure them!"[16]

His well-informed enthusiasm found its natural home in the early fifties, when the Blues Boy was one of the most popular disc jockeys on WDIA in Memphis. As a pioneer of African-American radio in the United States, WDIA was eagerly courted by record companies in the rhythm and blues field, who sent in heaps of records in the hope of obtaining airtime; in WDIA's record library, King could get to know what was being released at any given moment, albeit the choice was slightly weighted towards the Texas and West Coast artists who were the top sellers at that time.

The eclecticism of his music was foreshadowed by the diversity of his radio program, which ranged from Bing Crosby to Louis Armstrong, although naturally his preference was for his own heroes and heroines, like Ivory Joe Hunter, Big Jay McNeely, Dinah Washington, Sarah Vaughan, Louis Jordan, Roy Brown and Roy Milton.

In his time at WDIA, B. B. also acquired a deep knowledge of how to work an audience, and this experience was undoubtedly important in making him the showman par excellence that he has been for more than forty years. "I think one of the nice things about my career was part of the radio training. It taught me my technique, it taught me things about either too loud or not loud enough, even playing as well as singing, it taught me a little bit about projection, how to get an audience to listen, you know you have that imaginary audience when you are sitting in front of the microphone, you don't see them but you know they are there, then there are times when you figure that they aren't there. That helped me a lot."[17]

But even more than the eclectic influences, what makes B. B. King an original and enduring stylist is his approach to his instrument. This is especially remarkable when it is realized that his first ambition was to become a top-flight singer. His early recordings for Bullet and RPM make it clear that at first his guitar was no more than a backing instrument; not until 1953, when "Blind Love" marked the first appearance of that cunning blend of voice and guitar which is B. B. King's sound, was there any hint that he would revolutionize the playing of his instrument.

"When I first started, couldn't nobody tell me I couldn't sing. See, if you told me I couldn't sing then, I would have an argument with you. Later on, I found out how little I really knew, how bad it really sounded. I then found out that my guitar playing wasn't any good either. . . . My singing was more popular in the early years than my guitar playing. . . . I think my playing was very, very, *very* limited, more so than my singing, because I did have a kind of style of singing at that time."[18]

The notion that the guitar could take over from the voice at dramatic highpoints in his songs came to him gradually. As so often with B. B. King, his inventiveness and creativity were initially spurred on by a perceived deficiency. "When I first started playing, my co-ordination wasn't very good, so trying to sing and play at the same time didn't get to me. I'll put it that way: while I'm entertaining, while I'm trying to get my breath, or think of a new line to tell you, then the guitar takes over, until I think of what I'm going to do. If I'm singing, then I have to hit a chord and hold it, because I could never try to sing and play to myself at the same time."[19]

Thus King's genius lay in giving his guitar a vocal role and letting it sing the responses that had hitherto been laid down by the other solo instruments, usually the brass. At first, he had chosen the guitar mostly for lack of an alternative. "During that time, guitars hadn't really come into being, if you will. Excuse the word, but it was a bitch to try to get a good guitar at that time—just to try and get one. And when you did get one, you better hold onto it—don't loan it to nobody. . . . Where I grew up, there was no other instrument that was available to you, really, but maybe a harmonica. In my area, they couldn't afford keyboards of any kind."[20]

King was not the first guitarist to want to give the instrument a front-line role; his idols Lonnie Johnson, Blind Lemon Jefferson, T-Bone Walker and Charlie Christian had already done so in varying degrees. By chance, one of his friends was stationed in Europe during the war, and as a result King also became aware of one of the great single-string players, Django Reinhardt: "I think one of the things that made him [different] was because he started off studying to be a violinist, and due to an accident in his trailer he got his hand burned, [and] started playing the guitar. So now, when he started to play guitar, to me Django had a trill that he would get on his guitar. Each time he would hit a note, it was just like there was not going to be another one—so I'll take care of this here, and milk this one as long as I can. So each time he touched that [note] it was like touching a lady, you know; this is it! And I would feel that certain little something [when I listened to him], and I still do."[21]

B. B. also admired Django's romantic melody lines, which only pianists and wind musicians had managed to play hitherto. His aim was to reproduce on the guitar the lyricism of jazz players like the trumpeter Cootie Williams and the saxophonists Johnny Hodges, Ben Webster and Lester Young. "Even though they may be in different categories, even though some are jazz and some are blues, when I hear [other players] *phrase*, each note to me seems to say something. And it doesn't have to be sixty-four notes to a bar. Just one note sometimes seems to tell me a whole lot. So that's one of the reasons why I like . . . Louis Jordan; even though he plays saxophone, the way he phrases seems to tell me something, and that can just stop me cold when I listen."[22]

King says, "Listening to horn players after I started trying to play, I hear a guy playing and he phrases a note, in other words bends it like Lester Young used to do. . . . And I think this is the same thing I've tried to do on the guitar. It's been a sound that I've heard for years but I haven't got it exactly like I want it. I believe a guy should be able to phrase on a guitar almost like the singing of a violin or saxophone."[23]

For a musician trying, like B. B. King, to make the guitar sound as lyrical as the saxophone, there were already tried and tested techniques which enabled a player to produce long, singing lines. One of the characteristics of the prewar blues was the use of the almost Hawaiian-sounding slide guitar: the guitarist slides a bottleneck or metal tube over the strings at the neck of the instrument, producing long, flowing melodic lines which have more in common with singing than with traditional staccato chording.

B. B.'s cousin Bukka White was an expert slide player—though a staccato rather than a melodic one—whose exuberance fascinated the young Riley from an early age. Subsequently, slide guitar masters like Tampa Red, Robert Nighthawk and Elmore James who played long flowing lines made King feel sure that this was the style that best fitted his aims. His frustration was all the greater when it became clear that, despite repeated efforts, he could not master this difficult playing technique.

Several people have testified that King hoped for some time that he would be able to manage it. The singer Andrew Odom, who worked with the virtuoso guitarist Earl Hooker for a long time, reported that King admired Earl's slide playing so much that he even offered to pay to learn it: "That was at Kansas City Red's place on Madison and Loomis [in Chicago], and B. B. King came by that night and he asked Earl, say, 'Hey, man, why don't you teach me how to play the slide?', say, 'I'll pay you a grand a week if you teach me.' "[24]

"Earl Hooker, as far as I was concerned, was one of the three people that I loved their slides, with Robert Nighthawk and Bukka White. Earl Hooker was the more modern of all three, so that knocked me out. I was crazy about his playin'," King confirms. "I heard Elmore James before that, Bukka White, shall we say Furry Lewis, . . . and Kokomo Arnold! It was quite a few that I'd heard with the Hawaiian steel. But I'm sure that had I come along after Earl Hooker, I would have been influenced by him, because I liked his playing and I still do. To me he is the best of the modern guitarists. Period. With the slide, he was the best. Quick fingers, very fast fingers, and I used to tell him that he had fingers like Django [Reinhardt]."[25]

Rather than plugging away trying to master slide guitar, King eventually developed a technique which let him produce the slide sound he admired with just the fingers of his left hand. It was by chance, and once again in an effort to overcome a defect in his playing, that King created the style which has ever after been linked with him. "I never could play the slide like Bukka White, but I realized that by trilling my left hand, I could hold notes and get a sound that was close to that. So you might say that the way I sustain and vibrate my tones, that was inspired by people like Elmore James and my cousin Bukka White. But I'm still far from the sound that I would like to get, but I work on it every day. Now they tell me that I'm doing better," says King, with surprising but characteristic modesty.[26]

This modesty is also seen in the relentless way that King continues to study the playing of his instrument. It shows a remarkable humility in an artist of his status to decide that after all these years, and despite the unanimous admiration of his audiences and his peers, he still has a lot to learn. By the same token, there's a certain bravery, while he is playing an average of three hundred concerts a year, in finding the time to study harmony and composition through the rather dry Schillinger system. Dr. Joseph Schillinger, a former teacher of George Gershwin, was a noted theorist who paralleled music composition to mathematical principles in a famous method which King's friend, arranger Hampton Reese, introduced him to in the sixties.

Although he likes to experiment when practicing alone, King sensibly prefers not to take risks on stage, and sticks to thoroughly tested musical ideas. For a musician as shrewd as he is, improvisation is a skill that has to be worked on continuously, and only gets free rein in the recording studio, as he told Jerry Richardson, a student of his style: "T-Bone [Walker], I like to think, played what he knew and didn't experiment. In other words, what he played had been played in his room or was already in his head. . . . [Bill Jennings] seemed to be one of those people like Oscar Peterson and a lot of other people that play what they think. Anything they think, they play it. Now, a lot of us can't do that, and I am one. If you give me three or four bars to think about, maybe I can get it under my fingers, but

I don't play everything I think. I wish I could. . . . [But] when I record, everything is improvised. I never play anything that I planned to play. . . . I play exactly what I feel then."[27]

This total readiness to improvise when recording does have drawbacks; King is not immune to error, and one day in 1970, one of his wrong notes even achieved immortality. It happened at the end of "Chains and Things," which he was recording for inclusion on *Indianola Mississippi Seeds*. "I made a mistake," he confesses. "Now you're getting all the secrets. My bandleader and I have laughed about it many times, but I made a mistake and hit the wrong note and worked my way out of it. We liked the way it sounded, so we got the arranger to have the strings follow it. They repeat the phrase the way I played it. If you've got a good take going and then hit one wrong note, you don't want to stop."[28]

This feeling that one must be constantly striving for self-improvement, which King inherited from his parents and his teacher, Luther Henson, is the engine of his success, and the reason his style has remained popular. Unlike some musicians, who are content to spend their careers regurgitating the sound that first made them successful, King always tries to bring something new to his performances. "Well, it's kind of like every record I've made: I always thought there was something special on it. I've never made a perfect record, but each time that I played a record, I always felt that I played something that I never played before—even if I didn't like it afterwards. I think I am quite critical of most things I do."[29]

King has not been alone in undertaking this daily effort over the last several decades. His constant companion, Lucille, is there to share the best moments and the worst. B. B. King's story is also Lucille's; she got her name even before Riley became B. B., in the days when he was just developing his playing style. Lucille was born in 1949, in Twist, Arkansas, a tiny settlement of a hundred souls a few miles northwest of Memphis. King has often told the story of her birth, but the official version is the one that he recorded on the album *Lucille*. "It was during the taping session," Bob Thiele reminisced. "We were taking a break when I noticed B. B. doodling on the guitar. He was idling through some runs and started to tell me the story of 'Lucille.' I grabbed the switch, signaled the engineer, and flipped him on live."[30]

"The sound that you're listening to is from my guitar that's named Lucille. I'm very crazy about Lucille. Lucille took me from the plantation, or you might say, brought me fame. . . . A lot of you wanna know why I called my guitar Lucille. Lucille has practically saved my life two or three times. No kiddin', it really has! I remember once I was in an automobile accident, and when the car stopped turning over, it fell over on Lucille and it held it up off me, really, it held it up off me! So that's one time it saved my life.

"The way I came by the name of Lucille, I was over in Twist, Arkansas—I know you never heard of that one, have you? And one night, a guy started a ball over there, you know, he started brawlin', you know what I mean. And the guy that was mad with his old lady, when she fell over on this gas tank that was burnin' for heat, the gas ran all over the floor, . . . the building caught on fire, it almost burned me up, tryin' to save Lucille. Oh, I imagine you still wonder why I call her Lucille: the lady that started that brawl that night was named Lucille. And that's been Lucille ever since to me."[31]

Since the Twist episode, the original Lucille has become a great-great-grandmother several times over, with a whole series of descendants to her name. Some have been stolen; some were destroyed in car and bus accidents; some are living out their old age peacefully in blues museums; and some are stacked up in B. B.'s Las Vegas home. As a result, there have been almost twenty different Lucilles. The only thing that hasn't changed in a long time in this family tree is the maker of King's guitars; he has stayed true to Gibson. After trying various models, King found what he was looking for in the hollow-bodied stereo ES-355 first marketed by Gibson in the late fifties. "It was hard to get and keep a good guitar, so the early '50s is when the Fenders first came out. So I had one of the early Fenders. I had the Gretsch, I even had a Silvertone from Sears, Roebuck. . . . But when I found that little Gibson with the long neck, that did it. That's like finding your wife forever."[32]

In 1980, B. B. and Lucille received the ultimate accolade when Gibson decided to design a new prototype, inspired by the ES-355; christened "Lucille," it's now available commercially. Along with the jazz-pop guitarist Les Paul and the high priest of country music Chet Atkins, B. B. King is one of the very few artists to have a prestige instrument named as a tribute to him. It's just one more indisputable proof of his status as the leading light and personification of modern blues—together with Lucille, of course.

EPILOGUE

A biographer whose subject is still alive and well must be happy, even if his work is thereby rendered frustratingly incomplete. At the age of seventy-two, B. B. King appears to have no thought of retiring, though ill health has finally interfered as years on the road have taken their toll. Since he was diagnosed with diabetes in April 1990, King has had to cut down his traveling schedule to 250 dates a year, and he has been forced to change his stage show and start sitting down when he performs. Furthermore his doctors have strongly advised him to lose weight. By the turn of the decade, B. B. was about to reach the three-hundred mark on his weighing scale, and he is now spending a couple of weeks every year in a specialized Los Angeles institute in order to keep this problem in check. Clearly, this is the price to pay if he wants to remain active on the concert circuit.

For forty years he played three hundred concerts a year, not to mention the recording sessions, lectures, TV shows and film appearances that complete his daily round. As he proudly says, "I think it's the best time in my career this time. I can't remember ever being as popular as I am at this time. I mean, I can walk the streets now in most cities, and somebody will say, 'Hi, B. B., how are you?' And that used to didn't happen."[1] In this respect, his personal appearances and his seventy-some albums have been helpful, but so have the line of clothes and the food products bearing his name that Sid Seidenberg started on his behalf some time ago. Today, the name B. B. King is indeed more visible that he would have ever dreamed as a boy growing up in Mississippi. This is especially true in his home state, where a portion of Interstate 55 outside of the state capital, Jackson, has recently been renamed the B. B. King Freeway; closer to his home, in Indianola, there is even a new housing development called the B. B. King Estates!

A close look at the life story told here reveals that King has always bounced back, learning from his mistakes and oversights in order to go forward and break new ground. As far as he is concerned, any activity that advances the cause of the blues is a good one; to give a specific example, early in 1996 he ventured into interactive multimedia for the first time with the issue of a remarkable CD-ROM called "Down the Road with B. B. King," on which he takes us for an extended stroll through his story and that of his music.

It seems probable that while he is in good health, there will be other surprises in store for us. It's hard to imagine what this genial, creative Jack-of-all-trades might turn his hand to next. "There is just so much to do and so little time to do it," he told the African-American magazine *Ebony* at the start of 1992. "The day you've done it all is the day you die, and I'm not ready to die yet."[2]

On May 3, 1991, one of B. B.'s oldest dreams finally came true when B. B. King's Blues Club opened on Beale Street in Memphis. At the time, the Beale Street Management Association was trying to revitalize the area, and the presence of a large venue endorsed by the world's most famous blues singer was certainly an asset. "It feels great. I sometimes just sit back and think about it a little bit, like at night. . . . Lucille and me finally made it back home."[3]

The success of this venture prompted him to make a similar deal in July 1994, with B. B. King's Place, a four-hundred-seat club on Universal City Walk in Los Angeles. On three floors, this very fashionable nightspot offers blues and Memphis soul food to a high-class clientele. The actor Tim Reid celebrated his fiftieth birthday there with a blowout attended by all the big names in Hollywood, proving that the Mississippi blues had become the last word in style. Yet business always prevails, and it was learned during the summer of 1996 that Kingsid Ventures Ltd. (a company King owns with Sid Seidenberg) was suing the managements of both clubs for back royalty payments of over two hundred thousand dollars for the use of B. B. King's name. The dispute seemed to be related to the fact that B. B. was himself behind on the number of personal appearances he was committed to make at his clubs. The protagonists will eventually come to some sort of settlement, but the argument has delayed the opening of further franchised B. B. King clubs in Nashville, Orlando, and Seattle.

In the area of recording, after working with the great names and giving of his best, as he did with the *Blues Summit* album, King still has a career project he wants to carry out. "I wish I had time myself to make an album like a lot of the groups do. That is just spend weeks, months, two or three months. I wish I could do that once before I die."[4]

Asked to draw up a balance sheet of his life, King both recognizes modestly that there are more and better achievements ahead of him, and unaffectedly accepts that he has been a success: "I've been asked before if there was anything I would do differently if I had this life to start again. And there are only two things I can think of that I would change: I would finish high school and go to college and try to learn more about the music, and I wouldn't marry until after forty!"[5]

His lack of formal education troubles B. B., and he has tried to lessen its effects in all sorts of ways. He is also smart enough to realize that the problem is far from being his alone. He tries to find a solution for all those to whom life has not offered the opportunities they deserve, particularly in the African-American community. His will provides for part of his estate to be left to a number of educational institutions. "You know, I only went to the tenth grade, but the more popular I get, the more I feel the need for the education I didn't get."[6] In the same spirit, he supports MUSE (Musicians United for Superior Education), a program directed by his friend, the ethnomusicologist Charles Keil. Based in Buffalo, New York, MUSE seeks to develop creativity in school children through dance and percussion.

The other regret which usually comes up in interviews relates to his two failed marriages and his inability to give enough time to family life in general. "I've never been the father I wish I could have been and wanted to be. Due to my job, I just was never there in person. In spirit, yes, and financially, yes. I've been told by my children that just being there in person would have been better."[7]

When it comes to his children, the burden of guilt has often plagued B. B. over the years, but it became particularly heavy when Patty, the daughter he had in 1956 with a Florida club owner, was sentenced to nine years in jail for selling cocaine. Ever since he gave a free concert at the Cook County Correctional Institution in 1971, King has never stopped crusading for the rehabilitation of inmates. His appearance at the Gainesville, Florida, Community Correction Center in 1993 was all the more meaningful when *People* magazine and CBS revealed that among those who attended King's concert was his own daughter. For someone who is so reserved and who has tried to preserve the privacy of his children, it must have taken a lot of courage for B. B. to face the press that day. Not all of his offspring have wanted to keep their filiation secret, however; in addition to sons Leonard and Willie who have been part of his road crew, daughter Shirley is currently making a career as a vocalist in Chicago.

But children are one thing, and women are another. In a 1992 interview, B. B. spoke jokingly about wanting a companion for his old age: "[She must be] over twenty but not as old as I am at sixty-six. But she could be sixty-five."[8] Age and appearance are not unimportant to him, but, above all, a wife would have to understand and accept that he leads the life of a traveling musician; she would also have to refrain from being jealous either of Lucille, to whom he owes his career, or of the blues, for which he has given his all.

"Blues has always been a stepchild in the music business. People often put it down, and put you down if you played it. I've worked to change that. You've got to look and behave a certain way. My cousin Bukka White told me years ago, 'When you're going to perform, dress like you're going to the bank to borrow some money.' I tried to incorporate that attitude into my music as a whole. I've sacrificed for that. I missed out on my children growing up, didn't take them to the movies much. Both of my wives quit me simply because my head has been involved in that. . . . But that's the way it is most times when you're living a public life. And I've been lucky—my music has been accepted by more kinds of people and been heard in more kinds of places than any other blues."[9]

Even more than his guitar style, the worldwide acceptance of the blues which he has fostered may be B. B. King's chief legacy. In any event, that is his most ardent wish. "Long after I'm gone, when Robert Cray is my age, I hope kids will know what this music is all about and that it will be incorporated into the mainstream of music."[10]

NOTES

Introduction

1. Charles Keil, *Urban Blues* (Chicago and London: University of Chicago Press, 1966), 109, 111. King donated his impressive collection of records (four thousand LPs, seven hundred 45s and forty-four hundred 78s), films, tapes, and memorabilia to the Center for the Study of Southern Culture at the University of Mississippi in Oxford in the early 1980s, to become the core of their blues archive.

2. Stanley Dance, "Interview with B. B. King," in *B. B. King—The Personal Instructor* (New York: Amsco Pub., 1970), 12.

3. *The Arrival of B. B. King*, an authorized biography of King by Charles Sawyer, was published in the United States by Doubleday in 1980. An updated version of this work was recently released in Austria under the title *B. B. King Der Legendare Konig das Blues* (Vienna: Hannibal Verlag, 1995). The final chapter of this book, in its original English form, concurrently appeared in Britain's *Blues & Rhythm* (Charles Sawyer, "The Rise of B. B. King—Charles Sawyer reflects on the last fifteen years of the great man's career," *Blues & Rhythm* 106 [March 1996]: 4–8).

4. B. B. King with David Ritz, *Blues All Around Me* (New York: Avon Books, 1996).

Chapter 1

1. Rose Clayton, Bob Eagle, Bill Ferris, Mark Newman, Jim O'Neal, Suzanne Steel, "B. B. King," compiled by Mary Katherine Aldin and Peter Lee, *Living Blues* 80 (May/June 1988): 10 (hereafter cited as "B. B. King").

2. August Meier and Elliott Rudwick, *From Plantation to Ghetto* (New York: Hill and Wang, 1966), 77.

3. "B. B. King," 21.

4. E. Franklin Frazier, *Black Bourgeoisie* (New York: Collier, 1962), 23.

5. Paul E. Mertz, "Sharecropping and Tenancy," in *Encyclopedia of Southern Culture*, ed. Charles Reagan Wilson and William Ferris (Chapel Hill and London: University of North Carolina Press, 1989), 30.

6. Bruce Cook, *Listen to the Blues* (New York: Charles Scribner's Sons, 1973), 198.

7. Arnold Shaw, *Honkers and Shouters* (New York: Collier, 1978), 222.

8. "B. B. King," 10–11.

9. Jim Crockett, "My 10 Favorite Guitarists, by B. B. King," *Guitar Player* (March 1975): 22.

10. Dance, "Interview with B. B. King," 7.

11. Charles Sawyer, *The Arrival of B. B. King* (Garden City, NY: Doubleday, 1980), 115.

12. Sebastian Danchin, interview with B. B. King, Paris, France, October 24, 1991.

13. Sebastian Danchin, interview with B. B. King, Nancy, France, October 13, 1982.

14. Shaw, *Honkers and Shouters*, 218–19.

15. Danchin, interview with B. B. King, October 13, 1982.

16. Tom Wheeler, "B. B. King—Playing the Guitar Is Like Telling the Truth," *Guitar Player* (September 1980): 62.

17. Jas Obrecht, "B. B. and Billy—Memphis and the Early Years," *Guitar Player* (July 1991): 33.

18. Ibid., 26–27.

Chapter 2

1. Bengt Olsson, *Memphis Blues* (London: Studio Vista, 1970), 10.

2. "B. B. King,"13.

3. Obrecht, "Memphis and the Early Years," 26.

4. F. Jack Hurley and David Evans, "Bukka White" in *Tennessee Traditional Singers*, ed. Thomas G. Burton (Knoxville: University of Tennessee Press, 1981), 191.

5. Shaw, *Honkers and Shouters*, 220–21.

6. Pete Welding, "The Mississippi Giant," *Down Beat*, quoted in *B. B. King*, a promotional booklet published by SAS Productions (1981), 11.

7. Obrecht, "Memphis and the Early Years," 29.

8. Danchin, interview with B. B. King, October 13, 1982.

9. Peter Guralnick, *Lost Highway* (New York: Vintage, 1979), 60.

10. Obrecht, "Memphis and the Early Years," 27.

11. Louis Cantor, *Wheelin' on Beale* (New York: Pharos, 1992), 79.

12. Arnold Shaw,*The Rockin' '50s* (New York: Da Capo,1974), 97.

13. Cantor, *Wheelin' on Beale*, 79.

14. Shaw, *Rockin' '50s*, 97.

15. Dance, "Interview with B. B. King," 8.

16. Cantor, *Wheelin' on Beale*, 82.

17. Ibid., 152.

18. Dance, "Interview with B. B. King," 9.

19. Cantor, *Wheelin' on Beale*, 80.

20. Pete Welding, "B. B. King—From Beale Street to the World," in *Bluesland* (New York: Dutton, 1991), 197.

21. Ibid., 198.

22. Robert Palmer, *Deep Blues* (New York: Viking Press, 1981), 207.

23. "B. B. King," 17.

24. Ibid., 16–17.

25. *Billboard* (July 1949), in *First Pressings, Vol. 1–1948—1950*, ed. Galen Gart (Milford, NH: Big Nickel, 1986), 196.

26. Shaw, *Rockin' '50s*, 98.

27. Danchin, interview with B. B. King, October 13, 1982.

28. Sebastian Danchin, "Sam Phillips, Recording the Blues," *Soul Bag* 105 (winter 1986): 6.

29. "B. B. King," 15.

30. Guralnick, *Lost Highway*, 124.

31. Danchin, interview with B. B. King, October 13, 1982.

Chapter 3

1. Shaw, *Honkers and Shouters*, 204.

2. Ibid., 110.

3. Wheeler, "Playing the Guitar Is Like Telling the Truth," 69.

4. Shaw, *Honkers and Shouters*, 203.

5. Hal Webman, "Rhythm & Blues Notes," *Billboard* (February 1952), in *First Pressings, Vol. 2—1951–1952*, ed. Galen Gart (Milford, NH: Big Nickel, 1986), 512.

6. Leroy Bonner, "King of the One-Nighters," source unknown (1957), reprinted in *Blues Unlimited* 127 (November/December 1977): 18.

7. Shaw, *Rockin' '50s*, 99–100.

8. "B. B. King," 15.

9. Cantor, *Wheelin' on Beale*, 81.

10. Ibid., 84.

11. Ibid., 82.

12. "B. B. King," 14.

13. Sebastian Danchin, interview with Big Moose Walker, Chicago, Illinois, September 6, 1978.

14. Danchin, interview with B. B. King,, October 13, 1982.

15. Galen Gart and Roy C. Ames, *Duke/Peacock Records* (Milford, NH: Big Nickel, 1990), 24.

16. Giles Oakley, *The Devil's Music* (London: BBC, 1976), 234.

17. Wheeler, "Playing the Guitar Is Like Telling the Truth," 63.

18. *Billboard* (December 1954), in *First Pressings, Vol. 4–1954,* ed. Galen Gart (Milford, NH: Big Nickel, 1990), 128.

19. Bonner, "King of the One-Nighters," 17.

20. Shaw, *Honkers and Shouters*, 225.

21. *Tri-State Defender* (December 22, 1956).

22. Danchin, interview with B. B. King, October 13, 1982.

23. "Round the Wax Circle," *Billboard* (December 15, 1956).

24. Gart and Ames, *Duke/Peacock Records*, 110.

25. George A. Moonoogian, "Blues Boy's Kingdom," *Whiskey Women and . . .* 14 (June 1984): 30.

26. Ibid.

27. Ibid.

28. "B. B. King," 19.

29. Bonner, "King of the One-Nighters," 18.

30. "B. B. King," 18.

31. Gart and Ames, *Duke/Peacock Records*, 66.

32. Shaw, *Rockin' '50s*, 100.

33. Shaw, *Honkers and Shouters*, 222.

34. Shaw, *Rockin' '50s*, 101.

35. Ibid., 99.

36. Sawyer, *Arrival of B. B. King*, 77.

37. B. B. King, "Things I Don't Dig," *Rhythm & Blues Magazine*, reprinted in *Sun Records—The Blues Years 1950–1956*, Sun Box 105.

Chapter 4

1. Willie Dixon and Don Snowden, *I Am the Blues* (London and New York: Quartet Books, 1989), 207.

2. "B. B. King," 18.

3. Ibid.

4. Ibid., 18–19.

5. Bonner, "King of the One-Nighters," 19.

6. Fred Shruers, "Mississippi Homecoming," *Rolling Stone* (February 1990). 118.

7. Dance, "Interview with B. B. King," 11.

8. Ted Fox, *Showtime at the Apollo* (New York: Quartet Books, 1983), 215–16.

9. Keil, *Urban Blues*, 106.

10. Hurley and Evans, "Bukka White," 196–97.

11. Keil, *Urban Blues*, 102.

12. Sawyer, *Arrival of B. B. King*, 138.

13. "B. B. King," 22.

Chapter 5

1. Danchin, interview with B. B. King, October 24, 1991.

2. Ibid.

3. Ibid.

4. Ibid.

5. Bill Szymczyk, liner notes, *Live & Well*, BluesWay Bls-6031 (1969).

6. Alan Govenar, *Meeting the Blues* (Dallas: Taylor Publishing Company, 1988), 95–96.

7. "Rebirth of the Blues," *Newsweek* (May 26, 1969): 84.

8. Shaw, *Honkers and Shouters*, 521.

9. Govenar, *Meeting the Blues*, 96.

10. Jacques Demêtre, "B. B. King," *Blues Unlimited* 51 (March 1968): 3.

11. Govenar, *Meeting the Blues*, 97.

12. Val Wilmer, *Mama Said There'd Be Days Like This* (London: The Women's Press, 1989), 252.

13. Wheeler, "Playing the Guitar Is Like Telling the Truth," 82.

14. Joseph M. Comforti, "A Sociologist Talks to B. B. King," *Blues Unlimited* 64 (July 1969): 6.

15. "B. B. King," 20–21.

16. Ibid., 20.

17. Wheeler, "Playing the Guitar Is Like Telling the Truth," 76.

18. Ibid.

19. Michael Haralambos, *Right On: From Blues to Soul in Black America* (London: Eddison, 1974), 58.

Chapter 6

1. Sawyer, *Arrival of B. B. King*, 22.

2. Introductory monologue to "Don't Answer the Door," on *Now Appearing at Ole Miss*, MCA LP 452.

3. Danchin, interview with B. B. King, October 24, 1991.

4. On *Now Appearing at Ole Miss*.

5. Danchin, op. cit.

6. Dr. John with Jack Rummel, *Under a Hoodoo Moon* (New York: St. Martin's Press, 1994), 229–30.

7. B. B. King, liner notes, *Love Me Tender*, MCA LP 52125.

8. Danchin, op. cit.

9. Ibid.

10. John Landis, liner notes, *Into the Night*, MCA LP 5561.

11. "B. B. King," 20.

12. Danchin, op. cit.

13. Ibid.

14. Ibid.

15. Ibid.

16. Keil, *Urban Blues*, 111.

17. Danchin, op. cit.

18. Ibid.

19. Ibid.

20. Ibid.

Chapter 7

1. Gérard Herzhaft, *Encyclopedia of the Blues* (Fayetteville: University of Arkansas Press, 1992), 186–87.

2. Keil, *Urban Blues*, 108.

3. Cook, *Listen to the Blues*, 178–79.

4. Welding, "From Beale Street to the World," 187.

5. Ibid.

6. Obrecht, "Memphis and the Early Years," 33.

7. Ibid., 34.

8. Crockett, "My 10 Favorite Guitarists by B. B. King," 23.

9. Rob Bowman and Jerry Richardson, "Conversation with B. B. King: King of the Blues," *The Black Perspective in Music* 17 (1989): 150.

10. Helen Oakley Dance, *Stormy Monday: The T-Bone Walker Story* (Baton Rouge and London: Louisiana State University Press, 1987), 164.

11. Keil, *Urban Blues*, 107.

12. Bowman and Richardson, "Conversation with B. B. King," 139.

13. Welding, "From Beale Street to the World," 187.

14. Danchin, interview with B. B. King, October 24, 1991.

15. Shaw, *Rockin' '50s*, 100.

16. André Fonteyne, "B. B. King—The Blues Is Like a Mother Tree," *Soul Bag* 120 (summer 1990): 19.

17. Ibid., 20.

18. Wheeler, "Playing the Guitar Is Like Telling the Truth," 63–64.

19. Welding, "From Beale Street to the World," 197.

20. Obrecht, "Memphis and the Early Years," 33.

21. Bowman and Richardson, "Conversation with B. B. King," 150.

22. Wheeler, "Playing the Guitar Is Like Telling the Truth," 64.

23. Ralph Gleason, "B. B. King Interview," *Rolling Stone* (1968), reprinted in *B. B. King—The Personal Instructor* (New York: Amsco Pub., 1970), 16.

24. Sebastian Danchin, interview with Andrew Odom, Rennes, France, December 3, 1982.

25. Danchin, interview with B. B. King, October 13, 1982.

26. Ibid.

27. Bowman and Richardson, "Conversation with B. B. King," 144–45.

28. Wheeler, "Playing the Guitar Is Like Telling the Truth," 69.

29. Bowman and Richardson, "Conversation with B. B. King," 151.

30. Sheldon Harris, liner notes, *Lucille*, BluesWay BLS-6016 (1967).

31. "Lucille," on *Lucille*, BluesWay BLS-6016.

32. Obrecht, "Memphis and the Early Years," 35.

Epilogue

1. Danchin, interview with B. B. King, October 24, 1991.

2. Lynn Norment, "B. B. King Talks about the Blues and History," *Ebony* (February 1992): 50.

3. Ibid., 44.

4. "B. B. King," 20.
5. Obrecht, "Memphis and the Early Years," 35.
6. Norment, "King Talks about the Blues," 50.
7. Ibid., 46.
8. Ibid.
9. "B. B.'s Kingdom," *Down Beat* (February 1992): 18.
10. Norment, "King Talks About the Blues," 48.

SELECTED DISCOGRAPHY

This is a year-by-year listing of the songs recorded by B. B. King throughout his career. When known, references to 45s are followed by the date of release in brackets. Each time a song charted in *Billboard* magazine, the following indications are given next to its title: the charts concerned ("R&B" for black-oriented charts and "Hot" for the Hot 100), peak position for each chart, and the year the song peaked on those charts. For example: "The Thrill Is Gone **(R&B#3 & Hot#15 - 1970)**" means that "The Thrill Is Gone" went all the way up to number three and number fifteen respectively on *Billboard's* "Best-selling Soul Singles" and "Hot 100" charts in 1970. If, as in a few cases, RPM and Kent releases with the same reference number used alternatively two different songs on the flip side, the word "or" appears between the two B side titles (for instance, all records listed as RPM 451 had "Crying Won't Help You" on the A side, but on the B side some had "Sixteen Tons" and others had "Can't We Talk It Over").

1949	Bullet 309 (8/49)	Miss Martha King When Your Baby Packs Up and Goes
	Bullet 315 (10/49)	Got the Blues Take a Swing with Me
1950	RPM 304 (9/50)	Mistreated Woman B. B.'s Boogie
	RPM 311 (12/50)	The Other Night Blues Walkin' and Cryin'
1951	RPM 318 (3/51)	My Baby's Gone Don't You Want a Man Like Me

RPM 323 (6/51)   B. B.'s Blues
                  She's Dynamite

RPM 330 (8/51)   She's a Mean Woman
                  Hard Working Woman

RPM 339 (12/51)   Three O'Clock Blues (R&B#1 - 1952)
                  That Ain't the Way to Do It

RPM 348 (4/52)   She Don't Move Me No More
                  Fine Looking Woman

From 1951 sessions, released later on compilation albums:
                  A New Way of Driving
                  Questionnaire Blues
                  I Got a Girl Who Lives Up On the Hill

1952   RPM 355 (5/52)   Shake It Up and Go
                  (It's) My Own Fault Darling

RPM 360 (7/52)   Gotta Find My Baby
                  Some Day Somewhere

RPM 363 (8/52)   You Know I Love You (R&B#1 - 1952)
                  You Didn't Want Me

RPM 374 (12/52)   Story from My Heart and Soul (R&B#9 - 1952)
                  Boogie Woogie Woman

RPM 380 (3/53)   Woke Up This Morning (My Baby She Was Gone)
                     (R&B#3 - 1953)
                  Don't Have to Cry (Past Day)

From 1952 sessions, released later on compilation albums:
                  Low Down Dirty Baby
                  I'm So Glad
                  Pray for You

1953   RPM 386 (6/53)   Please Love Me (R&B#1 - 1953)
                  Highway Bound

RPM 391 (9/53)   Please Hurry Home (R&B#4 - 1953)
                  Neighborhood Affair

RPM 395 (12/53)   Blind Love
                  Why Did You Leave Me

RPM 403 (2/54)   Praying to the Lord
                  Please Help Me

Unissued sides recorded for Don Robey's Peacock label:
  Remember Me
  What a Difference
  I Don't Believe It
  I Can't Put You Down
  I Did Everything I Could
  I've Learned My Lesson
  Come On Baby Take a Swing with Me
  (I Want You to) Love Me

1954 RPM 408 (4/54) I Love You Baby
           The Woman I Love

    RPM 411 (6/54) Don't You Want a Man Like Me
           Everything I Do Is Wrong

    RPM 412 (7/54) When My Heart Beats Like a Hammer (R&B#8 - 1954)
           Bye! Bye! Baby

    RPM 416 (10/54) You Upset Me Baby (R&B#1 - 1954)
           Whole Lot of Love (R&B#8 - 1954)

From 1954 sessions, released later on compilation albums:
  Please Remember Me

1955 RPM 421 (1/55) Every Day (I Have the Blues) (R&B#8 - 1955)
           Sneakin' Around (with You) (R&B#14 - 1955)

    RPM 425 (4/55) Lonely and Blue
           Jump With You Baby

    RPM 430 (7/55) I'm in Love
           Shut Your Mouth

    RPM 435 (8/55) Talking the Blues
           Boogie Rock

    RPM 437 (9/55) Ten Long Years (I Had a Woman) (R&B#9 - 1955)
           What Can I Do (Just Sing the Blues)

    RPM 450 (12/55) I'm Cracking Up Over You
           Ruby Lee

    RPM 451 (1/56) Crying Won't Help You (R&B#15 - 1956)
           Sixteen Tons (*or*) Can't We Talk It Over (Come Back
            Baby)

From 1955 sessions, released later on compilation albums or Kent 45s:
I Was Blind
Baby Look at You

1956 RPM 457 (3/56) Did You Ever Love a Woman
Let's Do The Boogie

RPM 459 (4/56) Dark Is the Night Pt. 1
Dark Is the Night Pt. 2

RPM 468 (7/56) Sweet Little Angel (R&B#3 - 1956)
Bad Luck (R&B#6 - 1956)

RPM 479 (11/56) On My Word of Honor (R&B#3 - 1956)
Bim Bam

From 1956 sessions, released later on compilation albums:
Why I Sing the Blues

1957 RPM 486 (2/57) Early in the Morning
You Don't Know

RPM 490 (3/57) You Can't Fool My Heart
How Do I Love You

RPM 492 (4/57) I Want to Get Married (R&B#4 - 1957)
Troubles Troubles Troubles (R&B#13 - 1957)

RPM 494 (6/57) Be Careful With a Fool (Hot#95 - 1957)
(I'm Gonna) Quit My Baby

RPM 498 (9/57) I Need You So Bad (Hot#85 - 1957)
I Wonder

RPM 501 (11/57) The Key to My Kingdom
My Heart Belongs to You

From 1957 sessions, released later on Kent 45s and/or compilation albums:
I Stay in the Mood (R&B#45 - 1966, on Kent 450)
Bad Breaks

1958 Kent 301 (3/58) Why Do Everything Happen to Me
You Know I Go for You

Kent 307 (7/58) Don't Look Now, But I've Got the Blues
Days of Old

Kent 315 (10/58) Please Accept My Love (R&B#9 - 1958)
You've Been an Angel (R&B#16 - 1958)

Kent 317 (2/59)   I Am
                     Worry Worry

Kent 319 (3/59)   Come by Here
                     The Fool (A Fool Too Long)

Kent 325 (6/59)   A Lonely Lover's Plea
                     The Woman I Love (R&B#31 & Hot#94 - 1968, on Kent
                       492)

From 1958 sessions, released later on compilation albums:
                     Blues for Me (Groovin' Twist)
                     Looking the World Over
                     In the Middle of an Island
                     String Bean
                     I Love You So

Unissued sides recorded for Chess, released later on compilation albums:
                     Don't Keep Me Waiting
                     Recession Blues
                     Tickle Britches
                     Don't Break Your Promise

1959 to   Kent 327 (7/59)   Time to Say Goodbye
1961   Every Day I Have the Blues (with members of the
                       Count Basie Band)

Kent 329 (8/59)   Mean Ole Frisco
                     Sugar Mama

Kent 330 (10/59)   Sweet Sixteen Pt. 1 (R&B#2 - 1960)
                     Sweet Sixteen Pt. 2

Kent 333   (I've) Got a Right to Love My Baby (R&B#8 - 1960)
                     My Own Fault (or) Dry Bones

Kent 346   Partin' Time (R&B#8 - 1960)
                     Good Man Gone Bad

Kent 350   Walking Doctor Bill (R&B#23 - 1960)
                     You Done Lost Your Good Thing Now

Kent 351   Things Are Not the Same
                     Fishin' After Me (Catfish Blues)

Kent 353   Get Out of Here
                     Bad Luck Soul

Kent 358   Hold That Train
                     Understand

Kent 360	Peace of Mind (R&B#7 - 1961) Someday (R&B#16 - 1961)
Kent 362	Bad Case of Love You're Breaking My Heart
Kent 365	My Sometime Baby (R&B#27 - 1962) Lonely
Kent 372	Gonna Miss You Around Here (R&B#17 - 1962) Hully Gully (Twist)
Kent 373	Mashed Potato Time Three O'Clock Stomp
Kent 381	Mashing the Popeye Tell Me Baby
Kent 383	When My Heart Beats Like a Hammer Going Down Slow
Kent 386	Three O'Clock Blues Your Letter
Kent 387	Christmas Celebration Easy Listening (Blues)
Kent 388	Whole Lot of Lovin' Down Now
Kent 389	Trouble in Mind Long Nights
Kent 390	My Reward The Road I Travel
Kent 391	The Letter You Better Know
Kent 393	Rock Me Baby (Hot#34 - 1964) I Can't Lose
Kent 396	Let Me Love You You're Gonna Miss Me
Kent 403	Beautician Blues (Hot#82 - 1964) I Can Hear My Name
Kent 415	The Worst Thing in My Life Got 'em Bad

Kent 426	Blue Shadows (R&B#25 & Hot#97 - 1965) And Like That
Kent 429	Just A Dream (Dreams) [Why Do Everything Happen To Me, *recorded in 1958, and originally released on Kent 301*]
Kent 435	Have Mercy Baby Broken Promise
Kent 441	Eyesight to the Blind (R&B#31 - 1966) Just Like a Woman (Rockin' Twist)
Kent 445	Five Long Years Love Honor and Obey
Kent 447	I Wonder Why Ain't Nobody's Business
Kent 458	It's a Mean World (R&B#49–1967) Blues Stay Away
Kent 462	The Jungle (R&B#17 & Hot#94 - 1967) Long Gone Baby
Kent 467	Treat Me Right (Oh Baby) [Blind Love, *recorded in 1953, and originally released on RPM 395*]
Kent 470	Growing Old [Bad Breaks, *unissued 1957 recording*]
Kent 475	Soul Beat (Powerhouse) Sweet Thing
Kent 510	Shoutin' the Blues Your Fool
Kent 4526	Worried Life (R&B#48 - 1970) [Walking Doctor Bill, *originally released on Kent 350*]
Kent 4542	That Evil Child (R&B#34 & Hot#97 - 1971) [Tell Me Baby, *originally released on Kent 381*]
Kent 4566	Poontwangie Don't Get Around Much Anymore (*with the Tommy Dorsey Orchestra*)

B. B. King / With the Duke Ellington Band
　　　　　Yes Indeed

B. B. King / With the Southern California Community Choir (Crown LP 5119)
                    (Swing Low) Sweet Chariot
                    Precious Lord
                    Servant's Prayer
                    Jesus Gave Me Water
                    I'm Willing to Run All the Way
                    Save a Seat for Me
                    I Never Heard a Man
                    Army of the Lord
                    I'm Working on the Building
                    Ole Time Religion

B. B. King (Crown LP 5167)
                    (I've) Got A Right to Love My Baby
                    Good Man Gone Bad *(from Kent 346)*
                    Partin' Time *(from Kent 346)*
                    What a Way to Go
                    Long Nights (The Feeling They Call the Blues) *(from Kent
                      389)*
                    Feel Like a Million
                    I'll Survive
                    If I Lost You
                    You're on Top
                    I'm King

My Kind of Blues (Crown LP 5188)
                    You Done Lost Your Good Thing Now *(from Kent 350)*
                    Walking Doctor Bill *(from Kent 350)*
                    Fishin' After Me (Catfish Blues) *(from Kent 351)*
                    Hold That Train *(from Kent 358)*
                    Understand *(from Kent 358)*
                    Someday Baby
                    Mr. Pawnbroker
                    Driving Wheel
                    My Own Fault (Baby)
                    Please Set a Date

Easy Listening Blues (Crown LP 5286)
                    Hully Gully (Twist) *(from Kent 372)*
                    Easy Listening (Blues) *(from Kent 387)*
                    Blues for Me
                    Slow Walk (Slow Burn)
                    Shoutin' the Blues *(from Kent 510)*
                    Night Long
                    Confessin'

Don't Touch
Rambler
Walkin'

A Heart Full of Blues (Crown LP 5309)
Got 'em Bad
I Can't Explain
You're Gonna Miss Me
Troubles Don't Last
The Wrong Road
I Need You Baby
So Many Days
Down Hearted
Strange Things
Your Letter *(from Kent 386)*

From 1959 to 1961 sessions, released later on compilation albums:
Shotgun Blues
You Shouldn't Have Left
Shake Yours
That's How Much You Mean to Me
Who Can Your Good Man Be
Recession Blues
I Love You So
I've Got Papers on You Baby (Do What I Say)
Tomorrow Is Another Day
We Can't Make It
My Silent Prayer
Don't Cry Anymore
Slidin' and Glidin'
Blues with B. B.
King of Guitar
Jump with B. B.
38th Street Blues
Feedin' the Rock
Goin' South
Step It Up
Calypso Jazz
Swingin' with Sonny
Blues at Sunrise
Dust My Broom
Going Home
You Won't Listen
Sundown

1962   ABC 10486   Slowly Losing My Mind
to   How Do I Love You
1964
              ABC 10527   How Blue Can You Get (Hot#97 - 1964)
                                Please Accept My Love

              ABC 10552   Help the Poor (Hot#98 - 1964)
                                I Wouldn't Have It Any Other Way

              ABC 10576   Whole Lotta Lovin'
                                The Hurt

              ABC 10599   Never Trust a Woman (Hot#90 - 1964)
                                Worryin' Blues

              ABC 10616   Please Send Me Someone to Love
                                Stop Leading Me On

Mr. Blues (ABC LP 456)
                                Young Dreamers
                                By Myself
                                Chains of Love
                                A Mother's Love
                                Blues at Midnight
                                Sneaking Around
                                On My Word of Honor
                                Tomorrow Night
                                My Baby's Comin' Home
                                Guess Who
                                You Ask Me
                                I'm Gonna Sit in 'Til You Give in

Live at the Regal (ABC LP 509)
                                Every Day I Have the Blues
                                Sweet Little Angel
                                It's My Own Fault
                                How Blue Can You Get
                                Please Love Me
                                You Upset Me Baby
                                Worry, Worry
                                Woke Up this Mornin'
                                You Done Lost Your Good Thing Now
                                Help the Poor

Unissued (*) or released later on compilation albums:
                                That's Wrong Little Mama (*)
                                Rockin' Awhile

1965 ABC 10675 Night Owl
          Tired of Your Jive

      ABC 10710 I Need You
          Never Could Be You

      ABC 10724 All Over Again
          The Things You Put Me Through

      Confessin' the Blues (ABC LP 528)
          I'd Rather Drink Muddy Water
          Goin' to Chicago Blues
          See See Rider
          Do You Call That a Buddy
          Wee Baby Blues
          In the Dark
          Confessin' the Blues
          I'm Gonna Move to the Outskirts of Town
          How Long How Long Blues
          Cherry Red
          World of Trouble

1966 ABC 10766 You're Still a Square
          Tormented

      ABC 10856 Don't Answer the Door Pt. 1 (R&B#2 & Hot#72 - 1966)
          Don't Answer the Door Pt. 2

      ABC 10889 Waitin' on You
          Night Life

      BluesWay 61004 Think It Over
          I Don't Want You Cuttin' off Your Hair

      Bluesway 61012 Sweet Sixteen Pt. 1
          Sweet Sixteen Pt. 2

      Blues Is King (BluesWay LP 6001)
          (I'm) Waitin' on You
          Gambler's Blues
          Tired of Your Jive
          Night Life
          Buzz Me
          Don't Answer the Door

Blind Love
I Know What You're Putting Down
Baby Get Lost
Gonna Keep on Loving You

ABC unissued(*) or released in 1968 on BluesWay LP 6022:
Goin' Down Slow (*)
I Done Got Wise
Meet My Happiness

1967   *Blues on Top of Blues* (BluesWay LP 6011)
Heartbreaker
Losing Faith in You
Dance with Me
That's Wrong, Little Mama
Having My Say
I'm Not Wanted Anymore
Worried Dream
Paying the Cost to Be the Boss (R&B#10 & Hot#39 - 1968)
Until I Found You
I'm Gonna Do What They Do to Me (R&B#26 & Hot#74 - 1968)
Raining in My Heart
Now That You've Lost Me

Lucille (BluesWay LP 6016)
Lucille
You Move Me So
Country Girl
No Money No Luck
I Need Your Love
Rainin' All the Time
I'm With You
Stop Putting the Hurt on Me
Watch Yourself

1968   BluesWay 61022   Get Myself Somebody
Don't Waste My Time

Film Score: *For Love of Ivy* (ABC LP 7)
You Put It on Me (R&B#25 & Hot#82 - 1968)
The B. B. Jones (Hot#98 - 1968)
Messy but Good

1969　　　*Live & Well* (BluesWay LP 6031)

　　　　　　　　　　　I Want You So Bad (R&B#34 - 1969)
　　　　　　　　　　　Friends
　　　　　　　　　　　Get off My Back Woman (R&B#32 & Hot#74 - 1969)
　　　　　　　　　　　Let's Get Down to Business
　　　　　　　　　　　Why I Sing the Blues (R&B#13 & Hot#61 - 1969)
　　　　　　　　　　　Don't Answer the Door
　　　　　　　　　　　Just a Little Love (R&B#15 & Hot#76 - 1969)
　　　　　　　　　　　My Mood
　　　　　　　　　　　Sweet Little Angel
　　　　　　　　　　　Please Accept My Love

　　　　　Completely Well (BluesWay LP 6037)

　　　　　　　　　　　So Excited (R&B#14 & Hot#54 - 1970)
　　　　　　　　　　　No Good
　　　　　　　　　　　You're Losin' Me
　　　　　　　　　　　What Happened
　　　　　　　　　　　Confessin' the Blues
　　　　　　　　　　　Key to My Kingdom
　　　　　　　　　　　Cryin' Won't Help You Now
　　　　　　　　　　　You're Mean
　　　　　　　　　　　The Thrill Is Gone (R&B#3 & Hot#15 - 1970)

　　　　BluesWay unissued, later released on a compilation album:
　　　　　　　　　　　Fools Get Wise

　　　　BluesWay unissued, released the following year on ABC LP 713:
　　　　　　　　　　　Go Underground

1970　　　*Indianola Mississippi Seeds* (ABC LP 713)

　　　　　　　　　　　Nobody Loves Me but My Mother
　　　　　　　　　　　You're Still My Woman
　　　　　　　　　　　Ask Me No Questions (R&B#18 & Hot#40 - 1971)
　　　　　　　　　　　Until I'm Dead and Cold
　　　　　　　　　　　King's Special
　　　　　　　　　　　Ain't Gonna Worry My Life Anymore
　　　　　　　　　　　Chains and Things (R&B#6 & Hot#45 - 1970)
　　　　　　　　　　　[Go Underground, *from the 1969 "Live & Well" session*]
　　　　　　　　　　　Hummingbird (R&B#25 & Hot#48 - 1970)

　　　　　Live in Cook County Jail (ABC LP 723)

　　　　　　　　　　　Introduction
　　　　　　　　　　　Every Day I Have the Blues
　　　　　　　　　　　How Blue Can You Get

Worry Worry Worry
Medley: Three O'Clock Blues
    Darlin' You Know I Love You
Sweet Sixteen
The Thrill Is Gone
Please Accept My Love

1971   *Live in Japan* (ABC LP 131–2)
Every Day I Have the Blues
How Blue Can You Get
Eyesight to the Blind
Niji Baby
You Are Still My Woman
Chains and Things
Sweet Sixteen
Hummingbird
You Know I Love You
Japanese Boogie
Jamming at Sankei Hall
The Thrill Is Gone
Hikari N° 88

L.A. Midnight (ABC LP 743)
I Got Some Help I Don't Need (R&B#28 & Hot#92 -
    1972)
Help the Poor (R&B#36 & Hot#90 - 1971)
Can't You Hear Me Talking To You
Midnight
Sweet Sixteen (R&B#37 & Hot#93 - 1972)
(I Believe) I've Been Blue too Long
Lucille's Granny

In London (ABC LP 730)
Caldonia
Blue Shadows
Alexis Boogie
We Can't Agree
Ghetto Woman (R&B#25 & Hot#68 - 1971)
Wet Haystack
Part-Time Love
The Power of the Blues
Ain't Nobody Home (R&B#28 & Hot#46 - 1972)

Film Score: *Medicine Ball Caravan* (Warner Bros. LP 2565)
Medley: How Blue Can You Get

Just a Little Love
Please Send Me Someone to Love

1972   *Mar Y Sol Festival* (Atco LP 2705)
Why I Sing the Blues

Guess Who (ABC LP 759)
Summer in the City
Just Can't Please You
Any Other Way
You Don't Know Nothing about Love
Found What I Need
Neighborhood Affair
It Takes a Young Girl
Better Lovin' Man
Guess Who (R&B#21 & Hot#62 - 1972)
Shouldn't Have Left Me
Five Long Years

Newport Jazz Festival 1972 (Atlantic LP 9028)
I Need You Baby
Blue 'n' Boogie
Please Send Me Someone to Love

1973   *To Know You Is to Love You* (ABC LP 794)
I Like to Live the Love (R&B#6 & Hot#28 - 1974)
Respect Yourself
Who Are You (R&B#27 & Hot#78 - 1974)
Love
I Can't Leave
To Know You Is to Love You (R&B#12 & Hot#38 - 1973)
Oh to Me
Thank You for Loving the Blues

The Blues!!! A Real Summit Meeting (Accord LP 7212)
Outside Help (I Got Some Help I Don't Need)

1974   *Friends* (ABC LP 825)
Friends (R&B#34 - 1975)
I Got Them Blues
Baby I'm Yours
Up at 5 a.m.
Philadelphia (R&B#19 & Hot#64 - 1975)
When Everything Else Is Gone
My Song

B. B. King and Bobby Bland / Together for the First Time . . . Live (ABC LP 50190)
Introduction
Three O'Clock Blues
It's My Own Fault
Driftin' Blues
That's the Way Love Is
I'm Sorry
I'll Take Care of You
Don't Cry No More
Don't Answer the Door
Medley: Good to Be Back Home
  Driving Wheel
  Rock Me Momma
  Black Night
  Cherry Red
  It's My Own Fault
  Three O'Clock Blues
  Worried Life Blues
  Chains of Love
  Gonna Get Me an Old Woman
Why I Sing the Blues
Goin' Down Slow
I Like to Live the Love

1975   *Lucille Talks Back* (ABC LP 898)
Lucille Talks Back
Breaking up Somebody's Home
Reconsider Baby
Don't Make Me Pay for His Mistakes
When I'm Wrong (R&B#22 - 1976)
I Know the Price
Have Faith
Everybody Lies a Little

1976   *Bobby Bland and B. B. King / Together Again . . . Live* (ABC-Impulse LP 9317)
Let the Good Times Roll (R&B#20 - 1976)
Medley: Stormy Monday Blues
  Strange Things Happen
Feel So Bad
Medley: Mother-in-Law Blues
  Mean Old World
Every Day I Have the Blues

Medley: The Thrill Is Gone
  I Ain't Gonna Be the First to Cry

1977   *King Size* (ABC LP 977)

Don't You Lie to Me
I Wonder Why
Medley: I Just Want to Make Love to You
  Your Lovin' Turns Me On
Slow and Easy (R&B#88 - 1977)
Got My Mojo Working
Walkin' in the Sun
Mother Fuyer
The Same Love That Made Me Laugh
It's Just a Matter of Time

1978   *Midnight Believer* (ABC LP 1061)

When It All Comes Down
Midnight Believer
I Just Can't Leave Your Love Alone (R&B#90 - 1978)
Hold On
Never Make a Move Too Soon (R&B#19 - 1978)
A World Full of Strangers
Let Me Make You Cry a Little Longer

1979   *Take It Home* (MCA LP 3151)

Better Not Look Down (R&B#30 - 1979)
Same Old Story
Happy Birthday Blues
I've Always Been Lonely
Second Hand Woman
Tonight I'm Gonna Make You a Star
The Beginning of the End
A Story Everybody Knows
Take It Home

Now Appearing at Ole Miss (MCA LP 8016)

Intro: B. B. King Blues Theme
Caldonia
Blues Medley: Don't Answer the Door
  You Done Lost Your Good Thing Now
  I Need Love So Bad
  Nobody Loves Me but My Mother
Hold On
I Got Some Outside Help (I Don't Really Need)

Darlin' You Know I Love You
When I'm Wrong
The Thrill Is Gone
Never Make a Move Too Soon
Three O'Clock in the Morning
Rock Me Baby
Guess Who
I Just Can't Leave Your Love Alone

1980   *There Must Be a Better World Somewhere* (MCA LP 6162)
Life Ain't Nothing but a Party
Born Again Human
There Must Be a Better World Somewhere (R&B#91 -
1981)
The Victim
More, More, More
You're Going with Me

1981   *Live in London* (Crusaders LP 16013)
Every Day I Have the Blues
Night Life
Love the Life I'm Living
When It All Comes Down (I'll Still Be Around)
I've Got A Right to Give Up Livin' (All Over Again)
Encore

The Crusaders and B. B. King / *Royal Jam* (MCA LP 2801)
The Thrill Is Gone
Better Not Look Down
Hold On
Street Life
I Just Can't Leave Your Love Alone
Never Make a Move Too Soon

1982   *Love Me Tender* (MCA LP 5307)
One of Those Nights
Love Me Tender
Don't Change on Me
(I'd Be) A Legend in My Time
You've Always Got the Blues
Time Is a Thief
A World I Never Made
Night Life
Please Send Me Someone to Love

You and Me, Me and You
Since I Met You Baby

Blues 'n' Jazz

Inflation Blues
Broken Heart
Sell My Monkey
Heed My Warning
Teardrops from My Eyes
Rainbow Riot
Darlin' You Know I Love You
Make Love to Me
I Can't Let You Go

Unissued, released later on compilation albums:
Play with Your Poodle
Make Love to Me (Rehearsal)

1983   *Live from Midem, Cannes, France* (Kool Jazz LP 26001)
The Thrill Is Gone
Guess Who
Payin' the Cost to Be the Boss
Jam Session

Film Score: *The King of Comedy* (Warner Bros LP 23765)
'Tain't Nobody's Bizness If I Do

1984   *Six Silver Strings* (MCA CD 5616)
Six Silver Strings
Big Boss Man (R&B#62 - 1985)
Memory Lane
My Guitar Sings the Blues
Double Trouble

1985   Film Score: *Into the Night* (MCA LP 5561)
Into the Night (R&B#15 - 1985)
My Lucille
In the Midnight Hour
Enter Shaheen

1986   Film Score: *The Color of Money* (MCA LP 6189)
Standing on the Edge of Love

1987   Grover Washington, Jr., and B. B. King / *Strawberry Moon*
               (CBS LP 450464)
                               Caught a Touch of Your Love

               U2 and B. B. King / *Rattle and Hum* (Island LP 303400)
                               When Love Comes to Town (Hot#68 - 1989)

               Film Score: *Stormy Monday* (Virgin LP 2537)
                               Stormy Monday
                               The Thrill Is Gone

1988   Ray Charles and B.B. King / *Just Between Us* (Columbia CD 40703)
                               Nothing Like a Hundred Miles

               King of the Blues 1989 (MCA CD 42183)
                               Drowning in the Sea of Love
                               Can't Get Enough
                               Standing on the Edge
                               Go On
                               Let's Straighten It Out
                               Change in Your Lovin'
                               Undercover Man
                               Lay Another Log on the Fire
                               Business With My Baby Tonight
                               Take Off Your Shoes

1989   *Live at San Quentin* (MCA 6455)
                               B. B. Intro
                               Let the Good Times Roll
                               Every Day I Have the Blues
                               Whole Lotta Loving
                               Sweet Little Angel
                               Never Make a Move Too Soon
                               Into the Night
                               Ain't Nobody's Bizness
                               The Thrill Is Gone
                               Peace to the World
                               Nobody Loves Me but My Mother
                               Sweet Sixteen
                               Rock Me Baby

               B. B. King and Lee Atwater / *Red Hot and Blue* (Curb CD 77264)
                               Te-Ni-Nee-Ni-Nu
                               Bad Boy
                               Buzz Me
                               Knock on Wood

Life Is Like a Game
Red Hot and Blue

1990   Randy Travis and B. B. King / *Heroes and Friends*
(Warner Bros. CD 9 26310)
Waiting on the Light to Change

Bonnie Raitt and B. B. King / *Air America* (MCA 10677)
Right Time, Wrong Place

B. B. King and Sons Live (Victor CD 103)
Theme of Unusual - Blue Monk
Sweet Little Angel
How Blue Can You Get
Paying the Cost to Be the Boss
Guess Who
Double Deals
Everything Needs Love
Let the Good Times Roll
Feelin' Fine
The Thrill Is Gone
Caldonia
Darlin' You Know I Love You

Live at the Apollo (MCA CD 09637)
When Love Comes to Town
Sweet Sixteen
The Thrill Is Gone
Ain't Nobody's Bizness
Paying the Cost to Be the Boss
All Over Again
Night Life
Since I Met You Baby
Guess Who
Peace to the World

1991   *There Is Always One More Time* (MCA CD 10295)
I'm Moving On
Back in L. A.
The Blues Come Over Me (R&B#63 - 1992)
Fool Me Once
The Lowdown
Mean and Evil
Something Up My Sleeve

Roll, Roll, Roll

There Is Always One More Time

Gary Moore and B. B. King / *After Hours* (Virgin CD 2834)

Since I Met You Baby

Gary Burton and Friends, inc. B. B. King / *Six Pack* (GRP CD 96852)

Double Guatemala

Six Pack

Branford Marsalis and B. B. King / *I Heard You Twice The First Time* (Columbia CD 472169)

B. B.'s Blues

1993   *Blues Summit* (MCA 10710)

Playin' with My Friends (with Robert Cray)

Since I Met You Baby (with Katie Webster)

I Pity the Fool (with Buddy Guy)

You Shook Me (with John Lee Hooker)

Something You Got (with Koko Taylor)

There's Something on Your Mind (with Etta James)

Little by Little (with Lowell Fulson)

Call It Stormy Monday (with Albert Collins)

You're the Boss (with Ruth Brown)

We're Gonna Make It (with Irma Thomas)

I Gotta Move Out of This Neighborhood - Nobody Loves Me but My Mother

Everybody's Had the Blues (with Joe Louis Walker)

Gary Moore and B. B. King / *Still Got the Blues* (Virgin 921 472)

The Thrill Is Gone

1994   Diane Schuur and B. B. King / *Heart to Heart* (GRP 97722)

No One Ever Tells You

I Can't Stop Loving You

You Don't Know Me

It Had to Be You

All My Eggs in One Basket

Glory of Love

Try a Little Tenderness

Spirit in the Dark

Freedom

At Last

They Can't Take That Away from Me

1995   *A Tribute to Stevie Ray Vaughan* (Epic 485 067–2)

Telephone Song

INDEX

ABC Records, 58–61, 63, 66, 72, 75–77, 84–86, 90, 92–94

ACA Studio, 48, 49, 72

Ace, Johnny (John Alexander), 25, 30, 32, 34, 36, 40, 101

Ace Records, 58

Acuff, Roy, 96, 107

Adams, Arthur, 99

Aladdin Records, 27

Allen, Lee, 100

Allen, Steve, 84

Allison, Luther, 103

Allman Brothers Band, 81

Amazon Women on the Moon, 95

Anderson, Dorothy, 53

Anderson, Sam W., 11

Angelou, Maya, 77

Anka, Paul, 59

Ann Arbor Festival, 82

Apollo Theater, New York, 34, 64–65, 97

Aristocrat Records, 27

Armstrong, Louis, 5, 30, 74, 89, 106, 110

Arnold, James "Kokomo," 113

Associated Booking Agency, 75

Atkins, Chet, 115

Atlanta, Ga., 36, 38, 41

Atlantic City, N.J., 81

Atwater, Lee, 96

Autry, Gene, 107

Bailey, F. Lee, 88

Baker, Mickey, 82

Baltimore, Md., 29, 81

Barrett, Johnson, 9, 13–14, 21

Basie, William "Count," 12, 38, 44, 52, 53, 67, 97, 106, 107

Bass, Fontella, 76

Baton Rouge, La., 70

B. B. Queen, 103

Beale Street (Memphis, Tenn.), 15–20, 22–23, 29–30, 45, 82, 117

Beale Streeters, 30

Beatles, 81, 83, 84

Beck, Jeff, 103

Bell, Lurrie, 103

Bells of Harmony, 46

Belvin, Jesse, 60, 85

Bennett, Jack, 6

Bennett, Tony, 100

Benson, George, 84

Benton, Brook, 50, 52, 57

Benton, Buster, 103

Berclair, Miss., 1

Berkeley, Calif., 65

Bernstein, Leonard, 95

Berry, Chuck, 58, 103

Bethune, Mary McLeod, 5

Bihari, Joe, Jules, Lester, and Saul, 28–29, 32, 35–36, 48–53, 57–61, 79

Birmingham, Ala., 47

Bishop, Elvin, 80

Blackman, Phil, 91

Bland, Bobby "Blue," 29–30, 32, 36, 40, 56, 64, 66, 76, 85–86, 90
Blind Blake (Arthur Phelps), 105
"Blind Love," 36–37, 78, 110
Bloomfield, Mike, 80, 81, 103
Bluebird Records, 38
"Blues at Sunrise," 23, 108
Blues Boys Kingdom Records, 45–47, 86
Blues Boy Willie, 103
Blues on Top of Blues, 75, 77
Blues Summit, 99, 100, 117
BluesWay Records, 75–77
BMG Records, 98
Board, Johnny, 44, 46
Bo Diddley (Ellas McDaniel), 58
Bogan, Lucille, 38
Boston, Mass., 81, 88
Boyd, Eddie, 35
Boyz II Men, 32
Bracken, Jimmy, 40
Bradshaw, Tiny, 34, 63
Branch, Thomas and Ben, 27
Broonzy, "Big" Bill, 103
Brown, Charles, 50, 51, 106
Brown, Clarence "Gatemouth," 40, 42
Brown, James, 32, 57, 64, 66, 85
Brown, Ray, 97
Brown, Roy, 107, 110
Brown, Ruth, 32, 100
Brussels, Belgium, 98
Buffalo Booking Agency, 40–41, 43, 48, 63, 72
Buffalo, N.Y., 118
Bullet Records, 27–29, 110
Bumble Bee Slim (Amos Easton), 105
Burrell, Kenny, 97
Bush, George, 96

Callender, Red, 85
Calloway, Cab, 67
Cambridge, Mass., 65
Campbell, Eddie C., 103
Camp Shelby (Hattiesburg, Miss.), 9, 12, 73
Cannon, Gus, 17
Carr, Leroy, 107
Carson, Johnny, 84
Carter, Vivian, 40
Cartledge, Flake, 8–9

Cash, Johnny, 29, 87
Cauley, Ben, 100
CBS, 59, 118
"Chains and Things," 84, 114
Charioteers, 57
Charles, Ray, 32, 59, 76, 84, 93, 96–98, 100
Chess and Checker Records, 29, 32, 38, 49, 58
Chicago, Ill., x, 14, 18, 27, 32, 36, 38, 40, 41, 42, 51, 58–59, 65–69, 73, 81, 82, 87, 92, 100, 102, 104, 112
Christian, Charlie, 12, 106–07, 111
Clapton, Eric, 80, 101, 103
Clark, Dave, 78
Clark, Samuel, 59
Clarksdale, Miss., 11, 22, 28
Clayton, Dr. Peter, 37, 45, 107
Clearwater, Eddy, 103
Clovers, 32, 35
Club Ebony (Indianola, Miss.). See Johnnie Jones' Night Spot
Cole, Nat "King," 32, 35, 47, 50, 106
Coleman, Gary "B. B.," 103
Coleman, George, 25
Columbia Records, 57, 58
Completely Well, 78–79
Cooke, Sam, 52, 63, 64, 101
Cotton, James, 30, 80
Counts, Robert "Bones," 20
Cox, Ida, 67
Crawford, David, 94
Crawford, Hank, 93
Cray, Robert, 96, 103, 119
Crayton, "Pee Wee," 43
Creedence Clearwater Revival, 81
Crosby, Bing, 110
Crown Records, 57–58
Crudup, Arthur "Big Boy," 61
Crump, Edward H., 15
Crusaders, 92, 104
Culver City, Calif., 49, 72

Dallas, Tex., 36
Danny and the Juniors, 59
Denton, Martha, 10, 12, 14, 21, 24, 27, 31, 39, 53–54
Davidson, Pop, 3
Davis, Birkett, 7–8, 10

Davis, Jesse Ed, 85
Davis, Larry, 46, 86–87, 103
Davis, Maxwell, 51–53, 60, 76, 97
Davis, Miles, 25, 65
Davis, Sammy, Jr., 76
Decca Records, 109
DeCoteaux, Bert, 79
Demêtre, Jacques, 82
Detroit, Mich., 34, 66, 81
Diamond, Neil, 73
Dixon, Willie, 58
Domino, Antoine "Fats," 32, 36, 59, 62–63, 81, 96
"Don't Answer the Door," 62–63, 77
Doris, Walter, Jr., 7
Dorsey, Tommy, 52
Dotson, Willie, 12
Dr. John (Mac Rebennack), 81, 93
Dublin, Ireland, 96
Duke Records, 85–86
Duncan, Adolph "Billy," 30
Dylan, Bob (Robert Zimmerman), 89, 101

Eagles, 77
Eckstine, Billy, 62
Edison, Harry "Sweets," 97
Elkhorn Jubilee Singers, 7
Ellington, Edward Kennedy "Duke," 12, 34, 52, 67, 106
Emphrey, Calep, Jr., 91
Evers, Medgar, 1
"Every Day I Have the Blues," 37–38, 53, 68, 108

Fair, Rev. Archie, 6, 12, 104
Fairfield Four, 12, 104
FAIRR (Foundation for the Advancement of Inmates Rehabilitation and Recreation), 88
Famous St. John Gospel Singers, 10, 13
Farr, Elnora, 3–4, 7, 99
Fela, 83
Fender guitars, 115
Ferguson, Bert, 22–23, 27, 29, 34–35, 40
Figgis, Mike, 95
Fillmore Theaters, 81
Fitzgerald, Ella, 30, 67
Five Stars, 46
Fonteyne, André, 109
For Love of Ivy, 76

Forrest, Earl, 25, 30, 44
Four Tops, 63
Foxx, Redd, 34
Franklin, Aretha, 32, 54, 67
Franklin, Rev. C. L., 54
Freeman, Sonny, 66, 68
French Camp, Miss., 3
Fuller, "Blind Boy" (Fulton Allen), 103
Fulson, Lowell, 33, 36–38, 61, 76, 100, 108

Gainesville, Fla., 118
Garner, Honeymoon, 46
Gaye, Marvin, 32
Gershwin, George, 113
Gibson guitars, 19, 115
Gill, Leonard "Wine," 91
Gillespie, Dizzy, 65
Glaser, Joe, 74–75, 89
Glenn, Lloyd, 45, 76, 108
Golden Gate Quartet, 7, 13
Goodman, Bennie, 12, 106, 107
Gordon, Roscoe, 32, 36
Gordy, Berry, 40, 63
Gotham Records, 27
Graham, Bill, 80
Green, Al, 16
Green, Herman, 25–26
Green, Peter, 84
Green, Tuff, 27, 35
Greenville, Miss., 13, 41
Greenwood, Miss., 1–2, 13
Gretsch guitars, 115
Grimes, Lloyd "Tiny," 106
Grossman, Albert, 89
"Guess Who," 60, 85, 109
Guy, George "Buddy," 81, 100, 102–03

Haley, Bill, 109
Hall, Sue Carol, 54, 70–72
Hampton, Lionel, 25, 46
Hardy, Solomon, 25
Harris, Gene, 98
Harris, Sheldon, 75
Harris, Wynonie, 107
Harvey, Bill, 40, 42, 44, 51
Hawkins, Coleman, 52
Hawkins, Roy, 78, 108

Healey, Jeff, 96
Helena, Ark., 11
Henderson, Edwayne, 5, 8, 9
Hendrix, Jimi, 81
Henry, Robert, 30, 34
Henson, Luther, 5, 8, 114
Herenton, Willie W., 15
Herzhaft, Gérard, 102
Hines, Earl, 67
Hodges, Johnny, 112
Hodges, Mabon "Teenie," 100
Holford, Bill and Kay, 48–49
Holiday, Billie, 70, 96
Holloway, Red, 85
Hollywood, Calif., 76–77, 117
Hooker, Earl, 20, 29, 38, 103, 112–13
Hooker, John Lee, 25, 36, 51, 66
Hopkins, Sam "Lightnin'," 25, 36, 65
House, Son, 80
Houston, Tex., 36, 38, 40, 43, 72
Houston, Whitney, 32
"How Blue Can You Get," 61–63, 68, 87, 109
Howlin' Wolf (Chester Burnett), 11, 29, 36, 80
Hulbert, Maurice "Hot Rod," 29
Humes, Helen, 35
Hune, Dubois, 7
Hunter, "Ivory" Joe, 23, 100, 108, 110
Hurt, "Mississippi" John, 80

Imperial Records, 59
Impressions, 59
Indianola, Miss., 1, 9–10, 12–13, 38, 41, 44, 54, 116
Indianola Mississippi Seeds, 1, 84, 114
Into the Night, 94
Iron Butterfly, 81
Isley Brothers, 32
"It's My Own Fault," 51, 68
Itta Bena, Miss., 1, 13

Jackson, Miss., 45, 116
Jackson, Al, 20
Jackson, Rev. Jesse, 27
Jackson, Jim, 17
Jackson, Mahalia, 76
Jackson, Michael, 32, 95
Jackson, Russell, 91

Jagger, Mick, 81, 101
James, Elmore, 11, 112–13
James, Etta, 100
James, Nehemiah "Skip," 103
Jefferson, Blind Lemon, 5, 7, 45, 105, 109–11
Jemmott, Gerry, 77–78
Jennings, Bill, 106, 109, 113
Jennings, Will, 92, 99
Jerusalem, 84
Jethro, Duke, 66
Jett, Sammie, 27
Johnnie Jones' Night Spot (Indianola, Miss.), 11–12, 31, 41, 54
Johnson, Evelyn, 40–41, 43, 63
Johnson, Jimmy, 62
Johnson, Lonnie, 7, 105, 109–11
Johnson, Plas, 85, 97
Johnson, Robert, 26, 103, 105
Jones, E. Rodney, 69
Jones, Elvin, 82
Jones, Quincy, 76–77
Jones, Tom, 73
Joplin, Janis, 81
Jordan, Louis, 12, 27, 32, 45, 50, 58, 61, 92, 106, 109–10, 112
Joyner, George, 25

Kamp, E. A., 25
Keil, Charles, x, 65–66, 98, 102, 118
Keltner, Jim, 99
Kendricks, Belford, 60
Kennedy, "Tiny," 34
Kenner, Chris, 100
Kent Records, 57–58, 61
Kern, Don, 27–28
KFFA, Helena, Ark., 11, 21
Kilmichael, Miss., 2–4, 7–9, 83, 104
King, Albert (Albert Nelson), 101, 102–03
King, Albert Lee, 2, 7, 44, 54, 99
King, Bobby, 86–87
King, Carole, 84
King, Leonard, 118
King, Martin Luther, Jr., 27, 38, 65, 69, 87
King, Nora Ella, 2–4, 7, 99
King, Riley (B. B. King's uncle), 2
King, Riley B. ("B. B."): advertising and television, 74, 84, 94–95; children, 70, 118; education, x,

5, 8, 118; first guitars, 7, 8, 18; first recordings, 27–28; gospel music, 6–7, 10, 12–13, 57; health, 116; Lucille, 68, 76, 102, 114–15, 117, 119; movies, 76–77, 94–95; parents and family, 2–4, 7, 44, 54, 99; radio work, 22–25, 29–30, 39–40, 101, 110; touring, 38, 41–44, 47–48, 70, 82–83, 91, 97, 101, 116; wives, 10, 21, 24, 31, 39, 53–54, 70–72, 118–19

King, Shirley, 118
King, Willie, 118
"King Biscuit Time," 11, 21, 26
King Curtis (Curtis Ousley), 77
Kirkland, Eddie, 103
Knight, Gladys, 32, 34, 66, 73, 89–91
Kolax, "King," 38, 67
Kooper, Al, 77
Korner, Alexis, 84
KWEM, West Memphis, Ark., 21, 23

Lagos, Nigeria, 83
Lake Tahoe, Nev., 84
Landis, John, 94–95
Larsen, Neal, 99
Las Vegas, Nev., ix, 75, 79, 84–85, 90, 92, 109, 115
Lee, Milliard, 46, 50
Levine, Stewart, 92–94, 99
Lewis, Furry, 17, 113
Lewis, Jerry Lee, 29
Lexington, Miss., 7, 8, 99
Lieber, Jerry, 100
Liggins, Joe, 35, 43
Lincoln, Abbey, 76
Little Joe Blue (Joe Valery), 103
Little Milton (Milton Campbell), 29, 76, 100
Little Richard (Richard Penniman), 81
Little Rock, Ark., 46
Little Walter (Walter Jacobs), 35, 80
Live and Well, 77–78, 80
Live at Cook County Jail, 87, 97, 118
Live at San Quentin, 97, 104
Live at the Apollo, 97
Live at the Regal, 66–69, 75, 87
Lockwood, Robert, Jr., 11–12, 25–26
London, England, 83, 84, 92
Los Angeles, Calif., 27, 28, 36, 38, 40, 43, 44, 54, 60, 65, 72, 76, 81, 86, 95, 99, 100, 116, 117
Louis, Joe, 5

Love Me Tender, 93–94
Lucille, 76, 114

McClennan, Tommy, 37
McCrary, Sam, 12, 104
McGhee, Brownie, 64, 65
McKaie, Andy, 100
McLaughlin, John, 81
McNeely, "Big" Jay, 76, 110
McShann, Jay, 12
Mann, Herbie, 81
Marks, Miss., 11, 13
Martin, Dean, 50
Matthews, John and O. L., 10
Mattis, David James, 39–40
Mayall, John, 80
Mayfield, Curtis, 59, 67
Mayfield, Percy, 43, 76, 108
MCA Records, 93, 98, 100
Memphis, Tenn., ix, xii, 13, 15–26, 28–30, 32–34, 38–40, 44–45, 48, 54, 72, 80–81, 85, 96, 117
Memphis Horns, 100
Memphis Jug Band, 17
Memphis Slim (Peter Chatman), 38, 82, 108
Mercury Records, 58
Merrit, Jimmy, 46
Meters, 82
Midnight Believer, 92
Milburn, Amos, 51
Miller, Rice ("Sonny Boy Williamson"), 11–12, 21–23, 26, 36, 45–46, 61, 80, 104
Millinder, "Lucky," 44
Milton, Roy, 43, 110
Miracles, 64
"Miss Martha King," 27
Mitchell, "Sunbeam," 19, 42
Mitchell, Willie, 16
Mobile, Ala., 42
Modern Records, 28, 32, 35, 37, 43, 48–49, 53, 57–60, 63, 72, 77–78, 97, 108
Monterey Jazz Festival, 82
Moore, Rev. Dwight "Gatemouth," 30
Moore, Gary, 100
Moore, Johnny and Oscar, 51, 106
Moore, Max, 11
Moore, Winston, 87
Moorhead, Miss., 13

Motown Records, 40, 63
Muddy Waters (McKinley Morganfield), 11, 36, 80

NAACP (National Association for the Advancement of Colored People), 87
Nashville, Tenn., 93, 104, 117
NBC, 59
Nelson, Ford, 25
Nelson, Willie, 93
Newborn, Calvin, 27
Newborn, Ira, 94–95
Newborn, Phineas, Sr., 27
Newborn, Phineas, Jr., 27
Newman, "Fathead," 93
New Orleans, La., 2, 14, 15, 36, 41, 42, 82, 93, 100
Newport Jazz Festival, 65–66, 82
New York, N.Y., 18, 27, 34, 36, 59, 63–65, 72–73, 75, 77–78, 80–82, 84, 88, 90, 92, 97, 99, 102
Nichols, Alvin "B. B. Jones," 102
Nighthawk, Robert, 12, 20, 38, 112

Oakland, Calif., 65, 108
O'Daniel, W. Lee "Pappy," 11
Odetta, 64
Odom, Andrew "B. B.," 102, 112
O'Jays, 34
Onassis, Jackie, 84
Orlando, Fla., 117
Ory, "Kid," 76
Otis, Johnny, 40
Owens, Calvin, 91

Page, Jimmy, 103
Palmer, Earl, 85
Parchman, Miss., 1, 18, 104
Paris, France, 82, 98
Parker, "Colonel" Tom, 89
Parker, Herman "Junior," 29–30, 40, 42, 56
Parker, Nathaniel, 10
Pate, Johnny, 67, 75, 78
Paul, Les (Lester Polfus), 115
Peacock Records, 48–49, 58, 78, 85
Pepper, John, 39
Perkins, Carl, 29
Perry, Rosetta, 46
Peterson, Oscar, 113

Philadelphia, Pa., 64
Philip Morris Orchestra, 97–98
Phillips, Sam, 28–30, 32
Pine Bluff, Ark., 46
Pips, 73, 89–91
Pittsburgh, Pa., 98
"Please Accept My Love," 50, 87, 108
Poitier, Sidney, 76
Pomus, Jerome "Doc," 93, 99
Presley, Elvis, 17, 29–30, 45, 81, 89
Price, Lloyd, 32, 59, 63
Pride, Charley, 93
Prince, Roger Nelson, 95
Professor Longhair (Henry Roeland Byrd), 82
Pullian, William, 7

Rawls, Lou, 84
RCA-Victor Records, 57–58
Reese, Hampton, 113
Regal Theater, Chicago, 34, 66–69
Reinhardt, Django, 12, 111, 113
René, Leon and Otis, 40
Ritz, David, 101
Robey, Don, 40–41, 48–49, 85–86
Robinson, Fenton, 103
Robinson, Smokey, 64
"Rock Me Baby," 61, 104
Rodgers, Jimmie, 107
Rolling Stones, xii, 81, 96
Ross, Diana, 63, 70
Royal Teens, 59
RPM Records, 28–29, 31–33, 35, 37, 45, 49, 60, 96, 110
Rush, Otis, 102–03
Rushing, Jimmy, 62, 97, 107
Russell, Leon, 84

Sain, Oliver, 87
St. Louis, Mo., 14, 38, 87
Sample, Joe, 92, 104
Sanders, Richard, 25
San Francisco, Calif., 65, 80–81, 108
Saturday Night Live, 94
Sawyer, Charles, xii, 90
Schiffman, Bobby, 64
Schillinger, Dr. Joseph, x, 98, 113
Schuur, Diane "Deedles," 100

Scorsese, Martin, 95
Seals, Frank "Son," 103
Seattle, Wash., 117
Sebury, James Levi, 46–47
Seidenberg, Sidney A., 72–74, 76, 79, 84–85, 89–94, 97–101, 116–17
Shade, Will, 17
Shaw Booking Agency, 63, 72, 74
Silvertone guitars, 115
Simply Red, 99
Sinatra, Frank, 50, 62, 76, 85, 100
Singer, Hal, 82
Six Silver Strings, 94
"16th Street Grill" (West Memphis, Ark.), 22–25
Smith, Bessie, 34, 67
Smith, Rev. Utah, 7
Snow, Hank, 107
"Sonny Boy Williamson." *See* Miller, Rice
Southernaires, 7
Spann, Pervis, 67–68
Sparks, Milton and Aaron, 38
Spindel, Chris, 25
Starr, Ringo, 84
Stax Records, 16, 20
Stells, Jemimah, 5
Stokes, Frank, 17, 20
Stoller, Mike, 100
Stone, Henry, 94
Stormy Monday, 95
Strasbourg, France, 82
Sullivan, Ed, 84
Sumlin, Hubert, 103
Sun Records, 20
Supremes, 63
"Sweet Sixteen," 50–51, 53, 63, 78, 86–87
"Sweet Little Angel," 37–38, 50, 53, 68, 77, 86
Sykes, Roosevelt, 82
Szymczyk, Bill, 77–80, 84, 87, 92

Taj Mahal (Henry Fredericks), 85
Tampa Red (Hudson Woodbridge), 38, 112
Tatum, Art, 106
Taub, Jules. *See* Bihari, Jules
Taylor, Koko, 100
Taylor, N.C., 10
Temptations, 32, 63
Terry, Sonny, 64, 65

There Is Always One More Time, 98–99
There Must Be a Better World Somewhere, 93
Thiele, Bob, 76, 82, 114
Thomas, Irma, 100
Thomas, Rufus, 20, 29, 39
Thornton, Willie Mae "Big Mama," 35, 40
"Three O'Clock Blues," 31–35, 37–38, 41, 50, 53, 55, 63, 86, 87, 107, 108
"Thrill Is Gone, The," 78–80, 96, 108
To Know You Is To Love You, 85, 94
Tony! Toni! Toné!, 32
Townsend, Pete, 81
Trumpet Records, 45
Turner, Big Joe, 50, 62, 82, 107
Turner, Ike, 28, 32
Twist, Ak, 114–15
Twitty, Conway (Harold Jenkins), 93

Universal Attractions, 34, 40
USSR, 91
U2, xii, 96

Vaughan, Sarah, 110
Vaughan, Stevie Ray, 96, 100
Vicksburg, Miss., 2
Vinson, Eddie "Cleanhead," 82
Virgo Records, 86

Walker, Aaron "T-Bone," 51, 64, 76, 82, 106, 111, 113
Walker, Joe Louis, 100
Walker, Johnny "Big Moose," 41
Walker, James "Shinny," 44
Warwick, Dionne, 82
Washington, Dinah, 30, 100, 110
Washington, D.C., 34, 38, 41, 91
Washington, Grover, Jr., 100
WDIA, Memphis, Tenn., 22–25, 27–28, 30, 34–35, 38–40, 45, 106, 108, 110
Webb, Chick, 109
Webster, Ben, 112
Wells, Junior, 81, 100
West Memphis, Ark., 21–22
WGRM, Greenwood, Miss., 10
WGVM, Greenville, Miss., 10
Wheatstraw, Peetie, 107
"When Love Comes to Town," 96

White, Artie "Blues Boy," 103
White, Booker T. Washington "Bukka," 1, 18–21, 65, 82, 104, 112–13, 119
White, Josh, 65
White Citizens' Council, 1
"Why I Sing the Blues," 78
Williams, Clarence, 109
Williams, Cootie, 112
Williams, Joe, 38
Williams, Professor Nat D., 20, 22–23
Williamson, John Lee "Sonny Boy," 37, 104, 109
Wilmer, Val, 83
Wilson, Jackie, 52, 57
Wilson, James, 46
Wiltshire, Teacho, 61

Wingfield, Pete, 84
Winter, Johnny, 80, 84, 103
Withers, Ernest, 43, 45
Witherspoon, Jimmy, 35, 64
Wonder, Stevie, 32, 85
Wright, Billy, 36
WVON, Chicago, Ill., 67

X, Malcolm, 65

Young, Evelyn, 44
Young, "Mighty" Joe, 103
Young, Lester, 112

Zito, Louis, 73, 89